CQ's GUIDE
TO THE
U.S. CONSTITUTION

CQ's GUIDE
TO THE
U.S. CONSTITUTION

History, Text, Index, Glossary

Ralph Mitchell

Congressional Quarterly Inc.
1414 22nd Street N.W.
Washington, D.C. 20037

Congressional Quarterly Inc., an editorial research service and publishing company, serves clients in the fields of news, education, business and government. It combines Congressional Quarterly's specific coverage of Congress, government and politics with the more general subject range of an affiliated service, Editorial Research Reports.

Congressional Quarterly publishes the *Congressional Quarterly Weekly Report* and a variety of books, including college political science textbooks under the CQ Press imprint and public affairs paperbacks designed as timely reports to keep journalists, scholars and the public abreast of developing issues and events. CQ also publishes information directories and reference books on the federal government, national elections and politics, including the *Guide to Congress*, the *Guide to the U.S. Supreme Court*, the *Guide to U.S. Elections* and *Politics in America*. The *CQ Almanac*, a compendium of legislation for one session of Congress, is published each year. *Congress and the Nation*, a record of government for a presidential term, is published every four years.

CQ publishes *The Congressional Monitor*, a daily report on current and future activities of congressional committees, and several newsletters including *Congressional Insight*, a weekly analysis of congressional action, and *Campaign Practices Reports*, a semimonthly update on campaign laws.

An electronic online information system, the Washington Alert Service, provides immediate access to CQ's databases of legislative action, votes, schedules, profiles and analyses.

Library of Congress Cataloging in Publication Data

Mitchell, Ralph.
   CQ's guide to the Constitution of the United States.

   Rev. ed. of: An index to the Constitution of the United States, with glossary. 1st ed. 1980.
     1. United States — Constitutional law — Indexes.
I. Mitchell, Ralph. Index to the Constitution of the United States, with glossary. II. United States.   Constitution.   1986.   III. Title.
KF4528.5.M57   1986   342.73'023   86-2667
ISBN 0-87187-392-3 (pbk.)   347.30223

*To Osa, who waited patiently
and listened supportively throughout;*

*to Jill, who is far away,
working on a life of her own,*

*to Andrew, who is not yet
fully aware of what this is about;*

*to the Founders,
who activated the power in the People,*

*and to the People,
who must hold onto it,*

this is dedicated with love.

TABLE OF CONTENTS

EDITOR'S NOTE

In this book, the editors of Congressional Quarterly have joined with Ralph Mitchell to provide a handy and easy to use reference on the Constitution of the United States. Mr. Mitchell, as he explains in his preface, has created an index that allows students and other persons to find their way quickly to the constitutional provision of interest to them. To this, Mr. Mitchell has added a glossary that will help readers understand the terms used. The editors of Congressional Quarterly have supplemented this basic material with a brief history of the writing of the Constitution in 1787. This material, drawn from other CQ publications, constitutes the first half of the book and helps the reader understand the roots of the document that has been the basic law of the United States for two centuries.

PREFACE

Early one morning a political discussion started among some of my fellow teachers at New Trier West High School, in Northfield, Illinois. At one point, just before the bell rang for classes, a need arose to look up some provision or other in the Constitution. Then the bell ended the discussion. I have forgotten the provision, but the fact that there had been a need to look it up stayed with me. After searching for a reference book on the subject, and finding none, I began to realize that such a need must arise many times, and that it would be a useful tool. The United States Constitution is a magnificent document, remarkably simple and direct when one considers the stature of the system which it, in the hands of the Founders, set in motion. But it would be too much to expect that it could deal with both the complexities of the system and the problem of making all of its provisions and concepts easily located by those who want to know. On the other hand, any detail of a democracy's most fundamental law should be readily accessible to the people. It is better that the Constitution is admired up close than from a distance. So it was my first purpose to compile an index to fill this need.

As work progressed, however, two additional benefits emerged naturally within the index structure. One was that all provisions related to a specific major element of our government system collected themselves under main index headings, such as "States," "Congress," "House of Representatives," and so on. These topics are dealt with in so many articles and sections that there is no other way to focus on them than with the aid of groupings of provisions under main headings.

A second benefit was the opportunity to include important features inherent in our system: checks and balances, the federal relationship between national and state governments, due process of law, and civil rights and liberties. Under such headings are listed the references necessary to see how each feature was created.

Preface

Finally, it was because of such terms as "bill of attainder," "compulsory process," and "letters of marque and reprisal" that I felt that a glossary of the Constitution's terminology would be of help in understanding it further. I hope that joining the two — index and glossary — will help make the supreme law of our land more familiar ground and less awesome to behold, but no less grand.

Ralph Mitchell

WRITING THE CONSTITUTION

The 55 delegates who gathered in Philadelphia in the summer of 1787 faced a challenge of no mean proportions: How were they to devise a system of government that would bind 13 sovereign and rival states into one firm union without threatening the traditional freedoms for which the American colonists so recently had fought?

Americans, with their predominantly English heritage, were wedded to the principles of representative government and personal freedom, which had developed gradually in England from the signing of the Magna Carta in 1215. They had gone to war against the mother country to preserve their freedoms from the encroachments of centralized power.

But independence from Britain had brought new problems. Americans' allegiance still was directed toward their own states. The former colonists were reluctant to yield state sovereignty to any superior governmental power. The Articles of Confederation, the first basic law of the new nation, reflected this widespread distrust of centralized power. Under the Articles, the United States was little more than a league of sovereign states, bickering and feuding among themselves. The states retained control over most essential governmental functions, and Congress — in which each state had one vote — was the sole organ of central government. So limited were its powers that it could not levy taxes or regulate trade, and it had no sanction to enforce any of its decisions.

The inadequacies of the Articles of Confederation, brought into sharp focus by Shays' Rebellion in 1786, provided new impetus to an already growing movement for change that culminated in the Philadelphia Convention the following year. The delegates there voted to create a new national governing system consisting of supreme legislative, judicial and executive branches.

In the Constitution that emerged from these deliberations, the concept of government by consent of the governed formed the basic principle; accountability was the watchword. The rights of the people were to be protected by diffusing power among rival interests.

The Constitution strengthened central authority, but national powers were carefully enumerated; all other powers were reserved to the states and the people. The Constitution provided for a president, to be chosen by electors in each state, a national judiciary and a legislature of two chambers. The House of Representatives was to be popularly elected, while the Senate — which shared certain executive powers with the president — was to be chosen by the individual state legislatures. Under the terms of the so-called "Great Compromise" between the large and small states, representation in the House was to be proportional to a state's population, while in the Senate each state was to have two votes. The national plan finally agreed to by the convention delegates in Philadelphia, along with the Constitution's separation of powers between the three branches of government, created a system of checks and balances.

Writing in *The Federalist,* James Madison explained the delicate relationship between the federal and state governments and the division of power within the system. He stated:

> In the compound republic of America, the power surrendered by the people is first divided between two distinct governments, and then the portion allotted to each subdivided among distinct and separate departments. Hence a double security arises to the rights of the people. The different governments will control each other at the same time that each will be controlled by itself.

The final draft of the Constitution provided a broad framework for the new government. Thus for nearly 200 years the document has proved flexible enough to meet the nation's changing needs without extensive formal revision. Although many modern governmental practices would seem alien to the authors of the Constitution, the basic structure continues to operate in much the way they planned it. Madison realized the importance of "maintaining in practice the necessary partition of power among the several departments." This could best be done, he wrote, "by so contriving the interior structure of the government as that its several constituent parts may, by their mutual relations, be the means of keeping each other in their proper places."

Separate Roles of House and Senate

The House, because of its popularity with the people, was expected by Alexander Hamilton to be "a full match if not an overmatch for every other member of the government." The Senate was

---

Madison on the Constitution

"If men were angels, no government would be necessary. If angels were to govern men, neither external nor internal controls on government would be necessary. In framing a government which is to be administered by men over men, the great difficulty lies in this: you must first enable the government to control the governed; and in the next place oblige it to control itself. A dependence on the people is, no doubt, the primary control on the government; but experience has taught mankind the necessity of auxiliary precautions."

— James Madison, *The Federalist,* No. 51

---

originally designed to serve as a restraining influence on the House. But each chamber was given special power not shared by the other. The Senate's special authority over appointments and treaties was counterbalanced by the right of the House to originate all revenue bills.

At first the House, under the leadership of Madison and later under Henry Clay, was the pre-eminent chamber of Congress, but the Senate soon emerged as a powerful legislative force. In the years preceding the Civil War, it was the chief forum for the discussion of national issues, and in the post-Reconstruction era it became the dominant arm of the government. The House, as its membership increased, was compelled to adopt a variety of procedures that diminished the power of individual representatives but ensured its ability to act when action was desired. The Senate remained a comparatively small body, which found elaborate institutional structures unnecessary for the legislative deliberation that it saw as its paramount function.

In his book, *Congressional Government,* written in 1885, Woodrow Wilson stated:

> It is indispensable that besides the House of Representatives which runs on all fours with popular sentiment, we should have a body like the Senate which may refuse to run with it at all when it seems to be wrong — a body which has time and security enough to keep its head, if only now and then and but for a little while, till other people have had time to think. The Senate is fitted to do

deliberately and well the revising which is its properest function, because its position as a representative of state sovereignty is one of eminent dignity, securing for it ready and sincere respect, and because popular demands, ere they reach it with definite and authoritative suggestion, are diluted by passage through the feelings and conclusions of the state legislatures, which are the Senate's only immediate constituents.

Wilson's initial concept of the Senate, written long before he became president, might have been satisfactory to the framers of the Constitution, but in the 20th century it would no longer serve. As the Progressive era advanced, an increasingly restive public demanded more genuinely popular government, and in 1912 the Senate reluctantly agreed to a constitutional amendment providing for the direct election of senators. The House, too, felt the pressures of the times: the power of the Speaker that "Czar" Thomas B. Reed had established in 1890 was dismantled in 1910 under the banner of popular rule.

The Seventeenth Amendment, by taking senatorial elections out of the hands of the state governments, blurred the constitutional distinction between the Senate and House. From the time of the amendment's adoption in 1913, the Senate came more and more to resemble the lower chamber. At times it appeared to be the more representative legislative body. Both chambers, however, repeatedly have been subject to charges that they fail to represent the will of the electorate.

Although most members of Congress run for office today as Republicans or Democrats, the absence of unity within the national parties precludes party responsibility for legislative decisions. Moreover, the institutional characteristics of Congress itself often prevent a legislative majority from working its will. Campaigns in the 1960s and 1970s against the rigid seniority system, the Senate filibuster rule and secrecy in congressional committee sessions and in other activities all represented attempts to make Congress more accountable to the people. The same goal prompted demands for reapportionment of the House of Representatives to make congressional districts more nearly equal in population.

Congress and Presidential Power

The growth of presidential power in the 20th century, spurred by a major economic depression, two world wars and the Korean and Indochina conflicts, posed a threat to the viability of Congress as a coequal branch of government. As the volume and complexity of government business increased, legislative initiative shifted from Capitol Hill to the White House, and Congress with its antiquated procedures often found that it was no match for the tremendous resources of the executive branch.

By passing reorganization acts in 1946 and 1970 and a comprehensive budget law in 1974, Congress sought to restore its equality in the three-branch federal system provided by the Constitution. And repeated clashes between Congress and the executive branch over spending and the federal budget and the war and treaty powers reflected congressional resistance to what lawmakers saw as executive encroachment upon the powers delegated to Congress by the Constitution. One turning point was Congress' overriding of President Nixon's veto of the War Powers Act of 1973, the first legislation ever enacted that defined the president's constitutional role in making war.

Another power struggle, and ultimately a constitutional confrontation, between the two branches occurred over the Watergate scandal that drove Nixon from office. In June 1972 five men (two of whom were employees of the Committee for the Re-election of the President) broke in and attempted to burglarize the Democratic National Committee headquarters at the Watergate office-hotel complex in Washington, D.C. Although Nixon denied any knowledge of the break-in, he became implicated in the cover-up of the affair. Before its resolution after two years of sensational disclosures and mounting national agony, the scandal had tested the powers of the presidency, Congress and the Supreme Court. The Court played a crucial role by ruling unanimously that the president had no power to withhold evidence in a criminal trial. Nixon obeyed the court and surrendered the evidence — certain White House tape recordings — which led to House Judiciary Committee approval of three articles of impeachment against him and, 16 days after the court decision, to his resignation on August 9, 1974.

CONSTITUTIONAL BEGINNINGS

The state of the union under the Articles of Confederation had become a source of growing concern to leading Americans well before Shays' Rebellion shook the confidence of a wider public. In voluminous correspondence beginning as early as 1780, George Washington, John Jay, Thomas Jefferson, James Madison, James Monroe and many

Shays' Rebellion

The defects of the Articles of Confederation that were intended to bind together the newly independent colonies were massive. One of the most serious shortcomings was the inability of Congress under the Articles to help resolve a conflict between debtors and creditors that was aggravated by an economic depression and a shortage of currency after the Revolutionary War. Most of the states stopped issuing paper money and attempted to pay their war debts by raising taxes. At the same time, merchants and other creditors began to press for the collection of private debts. Squeezed on all sides, debtors (who were mostly farmers) clamored for relief through state laws to put off the collection of debts and to provide cheap money.

In response to this pressure, seven of the states resorted to paper money issues in 1786, during the worst of the depression. In Rhode Island debtors fared relatively well; many creditors, compelled by law to accept repayment in highly depreciated paper money, fled the state. But in Massachusetts, where the commercial class was in power, the state government refused to issue paper money and pressed forward with a deflationary program of high taxes; cattle and land were seized for debts, debtors crowded the jails and all petitions for relief were ignored.

Out of this turmoil came Shays' Rebellion of 1786, an uprising of distressed farmers in central Massachusetts led by Daniel Shays. Although the rebellion was put down by state militia in fairly short order, sympathy for the rebels was widespread. Their leaders were treated leniently, and a newly elected legislature acted to meet some of their demands. But the rebellion aroused the fears of many Americans for the future, and it pointed up another weakness of the Confederation — Congress had been unable to give Massachusetts any help. The rebellion also gave a strong push to the growing movement for governmental reform.

others expressed their fears that the union could not survive the strains of internal dissension and external weakness without some strengthening of central authority.

It was clear to Washington, writing in 1783, "that the honor, power and true interest of this country must be measured by a Continental scale, and that every departure therefrom weakens the Union, and may ultimately break the band which holds us together." He urged all patriots "to avert these evils, to form a Constitution that will give consistency, stability, and dignity to the Union and sufficient powers to the great Council of the Nation for general purposes."

How to form such a constitution was not yet clear. Opinions varied widely as to what would be "sufficient powers . . . for general purposes." Alexander Hamilton, in 1780, thought Congress should be given "complete sovereignty" over all but a few matters. But Congress had ignored proposals of its committees in 1781 that it seek authority to use troops "to compel any delinquent State to fulfill its Federal engagement" and to seize "the property of a State delinquent in its assigned proportion of men and money." While there was general agreement on congressional authority to levy a federal import duty, the effort to amend the Articles foundered on the rule of unanimity.

At Hamilton's urging, the New York Assembly asked Congress in 1782 to call a general convention of the states to revise the Articles. The Massachusetts Legislature seconded the request in 1785. Congress studied the proposal but was unable to reach any agreement. Then, Virginia and Maryland in 1785 worked out a plan to resolve conflicts between the two states over navigation and commercial regulations. This gave Madison the idea of calling a general meeting on commercial problems. In January 1786 the Virginia Assembly issued the call for a meeting in Annapolis in September.

Nine states named delegates to the Annapolis convention, but the dozen persons who assembled represented only five states — New York, New Jersey, Pennsylvania, Delaware and Virginia. Rather than seek a commercial agreement from so small a group, Madison and Hamilton persuaded the delegates on September 14 to adopt a report that described the state of the Union as "delicate and critical." The report recommended that the states appoint commissioners to meet the next May in Philadelphia "to devise such further provisions as shall appear to them necessary to render the constitution of the Federal Government adequate to the exigencies of the Union."

The proposal was deliberately vague. Madison and Hamilton knew there was strong opposition to giving the central government much more power. Some officials even preferred the alternative of dividing the union into two or more confederations of states with closer economic and political ties. Southerners were convinced that this was the ultimate objective of John Jay's offer to Spain to give up free navigation of the Mississippi in return for trading concessions of interest to New England. James Monroe, a Virginia delegate to Congress, saw it as part of a scheme "for dismembering the Confeder-

Twelve of the 13 Original Colonies ...

All of the states except Rhode Island (whose upper house balked) were represented at the Constitutional Convention of 1787, which met at the State House in Philadelphia from May 25 to September 15. The states appointed a total of 74 delegates, but only 55 attended, and their comings and goings held the average attendance to little more than 30.

Delegates

The 55 delegates who took part included many of the most distinguished men in America. Eight had signed the Declaration of Independence, seven had been governors of their respective states and 39 had served in the Congress of the Confederation. More than half were college graduates, and at least 33 were attorneys at law. Most of them had held prominent positions in the Revolutionary War, and all were well-respected men of substance in their states. A majority were under the age of 50 (five were under 30) and only four were 60 or over.

George Washington, then 55, and Benjamin Franklin, the oldest delegate at 81, were the most influential Americans of the time. General Washington, who had not wanted to participate at the convention as a delegate but had yielded for fear that his absence might be construed as indifference to the outcome, was the unanimous choice to preside at the convention. He took a limited but effective part in the deliberations. Those credited with the greatest influence were Gouverneur Morris and James Wilson of Pennsylvania, James Madison of Virginia and Roger Sherman of Connecticut, each of whom spoke well over 100 times.

Rules

The convention adopted its rules of procedure on May 28 and 29. There was some talk of the larger states getting more votes than the smaller, but the convention followed the custom under the Articles of Confederation in giving each state one vote. The rule provided that seven states would constitute a quorum. This rule was amended to permit reconsideration of any vote — a step taken many times during the convention. Reconsideration was made easier by a rule of secrecy providing that "nothing spoken in the House [was to] be printed or otherwise published or communicated without leave." Secrecy was essential, Madison wrote Jefferson, "to secure unbiased discussion within doors and to prevent misconceptions and misconstructions without." * The official journal,

... Attended the Constitutional Convention

limited to a report of formal motions and votes, was closed until 1819. Madison's shorthand notes, withheld until 1840, provided the fullest account.

Procedure

The convention began by moving into Committee of the Whole to debate the Virginia resolutions, which called for a national government with a bicameral legislature, an executive and a judiciary. The smaller states then rallied behind the New Jersey Plan, which proposed only modest revisions in the Articles of Confederation. After that plan was defeated June 19, the members reverted to convention, and a threatened deadlock was broken by the "Great Compromise" of July 16 giving each state an equal vote in the Senate. On July 24 a Committee of Detail (Nathaniel Gorham, Oliver Ellsworth, Edmund Randolph, John Rutledge and Wilson) was appointed to draft a constitution based on agreements already reached. The convention then took a ten-day recess during which Washington went fishing near Valley Forge. On September 8 a Committee of Style was named to polish the wording and arrange the articles. The final document was put before the convention on September 17.

The Signing

At this point, Franklin said he hoped "every member of the Convention who may still have objections to it [the Constitution], would, with me, on this occasion doubt a little of his own infallibility, and ... put his name to this instrument." ** He moved that the Constitution be signed by the unanimous consent of the states present. The motion was approved as was one change increasing representation in the House from one member for every 40,000 inhabitants to one for every 30,000 — a change supported by Washington in his only speech at the convention. The Constitution was signed by all but three of the 42 delegates still in attendance: George Mason, Edmund Randolph and Elbridge Gerry. After agreeing that the Constitution should be submitted to special conventions of the states for ratification, the convention adjourned.

*Charles Warren, *The Making of the Constitution* (Boston: Little, Brown & Co., 1928), p. 135.
** Ibid., p. 709.

acy and throwing the states eastward of the Hudson into one government."

The Virginia Assembly, prodded by Madison and Washington, agreed on October 16, 1786, to send delegates to Philadelphia, and six other states took similar action before Congress, on February 21, 1787, moved to retain control of the situation. It passed a resolution endorsing the proposed convention for the purpose of reporting to Congress and the several legislatures on its recommendations. Officially, therefore, the convention was to be no more than advisory to Congress.

Soon after the Philadelphia convention opened on May 25, 1787, the delegates were asked to decide whether to try to patch up the Articles of Confederation or to ignore them and draw up a new plan of government.

Congress, the state legislatures and many of the delegates expected the session in Philadelphia to do no more than draft proposals to revise the Articles in a way that would somehow strengthen the Confederation without altering the system of state sovereignty. But Madison and others who had worked to bring about the convention were convinced of the need for fundamental reform.

The Virginia Plan

These nationalists had come prepared, and on May 29 they seized the initiative. Edmund Randolph, acting for the Virginians, introduced 15 resolutions that added up to a plan for a new "National Government" of broad powers. The Virginia Plan called for a "National Legislature" of two houses, one to be elected by the people and the other by members of the first; a "National Executive" to be chosen by the Legislature; and a "National Judiciary." The Legislature would have power to legislate in all cases where the states were "incompetent" or would interrupt "the harmony of the United States," and to "negate" state laws contrary to the articles of union. And the states would be represented in both chambers in proportion to their wealth or their white population.

The convention moved at once into Committee of the Whole to consider the Randolph resolutions. The proposals clearly envisaged a central government that, unlike that of the Confederation, would operate directly upon the people and independently of the states. It was to be a "national government" in contrast to the "merely federal" system that had been tried and found wanting. What the Virginians had in mind, though, was a system in which national and state governments would exercise dual sovereignty over the people within

Legislative Nomenclature

The Constitutional Convention continued to speak of the "Legislature of the United States" and its "first branch" and "second branch" until those terms were changed in the August 6 report of the Committee of Detail to the "Congress of the United States," the "House of Representatives" and the "Senate." The term "Congress" was taken from the Articles of Confederation. "House of Representatives" was the name of the first branch in five states (the others being called the Assembly, House of Delegates and House of Commons). The second branch was called the "Senate" in all but two states.

Provisions of the Constitution relating to both the House and Senate referred to "each House" in keeping with English usage. But the terms "upper house" and "lower house" to denote the Senate and the House, which also were taken from English usage, were not included in the Constitution.

separate and prescribed fields. Randolph said that his plan "only means to give the national government power to defend and protect itself — to take, therefore, from the respective legislatures of states no more sovereignty than is competent to this end."

Such a dual system was unknown in 1787. To many delegates the term "national government" implied a unitary or consolidated regime of potentially unlimited powers that would extinguish the independence of the states. However, on May 30, with only Connecticut opposed and New York divided, they adopted Randolph's proposition "that a National Government ought to be established consisting of a supreme Legislative, Executive and Judiciary." This opening commitment by most of the delegates then present reflected the air of crisis in which they met.

The next step of the Committee of the Whole was to take up and approve several of the specific proposals of the Virginia Plan. As the debate proceeded, some members from smaller states became alarmed by the insistence of the larger states on proportional representation in both houses of the proposed national Legislature. Under one formula, Virginia, Pennsylvania and Massachusetts — the three most populous states — would have held 13 of 28 seats in the Senate as well as a similar share of seats in the House. This spelled domination to those accustomed to the equality of states that prevailed in the Congress of the Confederation and in the convention as well.

To Luther Martin of Maryland, such a plan meant "a system of slavery which bound hand and foot 10 states of the Union and placed them at the mercy of the other three." John Dickinson declared that "we would rather submit to a foreign power than submit to be deprived of an equality of suffrage in both branches of the Legislature, and thereby be thrown under the domination of the large states." New Jersey would "never confederate" on such a basis, said William Paterson, for "she would be swallowed up." He would "rather submit to a monarch, to a despot, than to such a fate."

The New Jersey Plan

On June 11 the convention voted six states to five to constitute the Senate on the same proportional basis as the House. That decision led Paterson and others to draft a purely federal alternative to the Virginia Plan. The New Jersey Plan, presented June 15, proposed amending the Articles of Confederation to give Congress authority to levy import duties and to regulate trade. It would have provided also for a plural executive, to be chosen by Congress, and a federal judiciary. It proposed that treaties and acts of Congress "shall be the supreme law," and that the executive be authorized to "call forth the power of the Confederated States" to enforce the laws if necessary. But the plan would have left each state with an equal voice in Congress and most of the attributes of sovereignty.

Paterson argued that his plan "accorded first with the powers of the convention, and second with the sentiments of the people. . . . Our object is not such a Government as may be best in itself, but such a one as our constituents have authorized us to prepare and as they will approve."

The nationalists rejected this concept of their responsibility. Randolph said he was not "scrupulous on the point of power. When the Republic was at stake, it would be treason to our trust not to propose what we found necessary." As Hamilton put it, the Union was in peril, and "to rely on and propose any plan not adequate to these exigencies, merely because it was not clearly within our powers, would be to sacrifice the means to the end. . . . The great question is what provisions shall we make for the happiness of our country?"

Madison was the last to speak against the New Jersey Plan, pointing up serious problems of the Confederation for which it offered no solution. On June 19 the delegates were asked to decide whether the

Randolph resolutions "should be adhered to as preferable to those of Mr. Paterson." Seven states voted yes and only three states no. That settled the issue of partial vs. total reform; a clear majority of the delegates were now committed to abandoning the Articles and to drafting a new constitution.

The Great Compromise

The task was to take three months. There were few points of unanimity among the 55 men participating. Delegates from the same state frequently were divided; as a result, states occasionally were unable to cast votes on constitutional proposals. The records of the convention also reveal that, although the nationalists won over a majority to their cause at an early stage, the original Virginia Plan was unacceptable in many of its details. The Constitution could not have been written without some degree of willingness on all sides to compromise in the interests of designing a workable and acceptable plan.

This became evident soon after defeat of the New Jersey Plan when the small states continued to demand and the large states to oppose equal representation in the Senate. On July 1 the convention split five to five on this issue. Faced with a deadlock, the convention named a committee to seek a compromise. It proposed on July 5 that, in return for equality of state representation in the Senate, the House be given sole power to originate money bills, which the Senate could accept or reject but not modify. This formula was finally approved July 16, five states to four, with Massachusetts divided and New York not voting because two of its three delegates had departed, never to return. On July 24 a five-member Committee of Detail was appointed to draft the Constitution according to the resolutions adopted by the convention. The draft presented August 6 included changes and additions that were refined through the following month. On September 8 another committee was named to revise the style and arrange the articles.

Without the Great Compromise the convention would have collapsed. As Madison pointed out, however, "the great division of interests" in America was not between the large and small but between the northern and southern states, partly because of climate but "principally from the effects of having or not having slaves." Although the southerners were mostly supporters of a strong central government, they were determined to limit its power to discriminate against the South's special interests in slavery, agricultural exports and western expansion. This stand necessitated other compromises that accounted for some of the key provisions of the new plan of government.

What finally emerged September 17 as the Constitution of the United States was a unique blend of national and federal systems based on republican principles of representative and limited government. It met the basic objective of the nationalists by providing for a central government of ample powers that could function independently of the states. It also met the concerns of states' rights supporters by surrounding that government with checks and balances to prevent the tyranny of any one branch.

The text of the Constitution does not follow the order in which the separate provisions were developed. The convention moved generally from decisions on broad principles to questions of detail and precision. But the interdependent nature of the various parts of the plan made for frequent reconsideration of decisions in one area to take account of subsequent decisions in another but related area. As a result, many of the provisions were altered or added in the final weeks of the convention. How the major provisions were developed is described in the following material.

THE STRUCTURE OF CONGRESS

The convention's early decision that a national government, if formed, should consist of three branches — legislative, executive and judicial — was undisputed. This division of governmental functions had been recognized from early colonial times and was reflected in most of the state constitutions. The failure of the Articles of Confederation to separate the functions was generally recognized as a serious mistake. The decision by the convention in favor of three branches of government also implied broad acceptance of the principle of separation of powers, although most of the provisions of the Constitution that gave effect to this principle were adopted on practical rather than theoretical grounds.

The Virginia Plan had called for a national legislature of two houses, according to the practice initiated by the English Parliament and followed by most of the colonial governments and retained by 10 of the 13 states. The Continental Congress and the Congress of the Articles of Confederation were unicameral, but once the convention had decided to abandon the Articles there was little question that the new Congress should be bicameral. As George Mason saw it, the minds of

Americans were settled on two points — "an attachment to republican government [and] an attachment to more than one branch in the Legislature." Only Pennsylvania dissented when the Committee of the Whole voted for two houses, and the convention confirmed the committee's decision June 21 by a vote of seven states to three.

Election to the House

The nationalists insisted that the new government rest on the consent of the people rather than on the state legislatures. They felt it was essential that at least "the first branch," the House, be elected "by the people immediately," as James Madison put it. The government "ought to possess . . . the mind or sense of the people at large," said James Wilson, and for that reason "the Legislature ought to be the most exact transcript of the whole society." The House "was to be the grand depository of the democratic principles of the Government," George Mason declared.

Those who were suspicious of a national government preferred election of the House by the state legislatures. "The people immediately should have as little to do" with electing the government as possible, according to Roger Sherman, because "they want information and are constantly liable to be misled." Elbridge Gerry was convinced that "the evils we experience flow from the excess of democracy," while Charles Pinckney thought "the people were less fit judges" than the legislatures to choose members of the House. The proposal for election by state legislatures twice was defeated, however, and popular election of the House was confirmed June 21 by a vote of nine states to one.

Election to the Senate

The Virginia Plan proposed that the House elect the "second branch" from persons nominated by the state legislatures. Few delegates supported this plan because it would have made the Senate subservient to the House. Most agreed with Gouverneur Morris that the Senate should "check the precipitation, changeableness and excesses of the first branch." (The concept of the Senate's role as that of representing the states emerged later, after the decision in favor of equal representation.) Neither was there any support for Madison's and Wilson's view that the people should elect the Senate as well as the House. Election of senators by the state legislatures was carried unanimously in the Committee of the Whole on June 7 and confirmed June 25 by a convention vote of nine states to two.

Basis of Representation

The Virginia Plan called for representation of the states in both the House and Senate in proportion to their wealth or free population. This proposal led to the revolt of the small states, which feared domination by the more wealthy and populous states. The matter was resolved by a vote on July 16 for equal representation of the states in the Senate. While the principle of proportional representation in the House was never seriously challenged, the idea of basing Senate representation on wealth or the free population raised numerous questions and led to adoption of important qualifications.

To retain southern support for proportional representation in the Senate, Wilson had proposed on June 11 that the House be apportioned according to a count of the whole number of free citizens and three-fifths of all others (meaning slaves), excluding Indians not paying taxes. This formula (first proposed in Congress in 1783) was adopted with only New Jersey and Delaware opposed. Then on July 9 the convention decided that the new Congress should have the power "to regulate the number of representatives upon the principles of wealth and number of inhabitants." Since southerners regarded slaves as property, this led northerners who wanted representation in the House to be based on population alone to ask why slaves should be counted at all.

As a result, on July 11 the convention voted six states to four to exclude blacks from the formula worked out June 11. At this point Gouverneur Morris proposed that the power of Congress to apportion the House according to wealth and numbers be subject to a proviso "that direct taxation shall be in proportion to representation." This proviso, which was adopted without debate, cast the slave issue in a different light: the South would have to pay additional taxes for any increases in representation it gained by counting slaves. The northerners then dropped their opposition to the three-fifths count demanded by the southerners, and on July 13 the convention restored that provision.

Because it was agreed finally that representation was to be based solely on population (counting all whites and three-fifths of the blacks), the word "wealth" was deleted from the provision adopted July 9. This solution to the issue gave five free voters in a slave state a voice in the House equivalent to that of seven free voters in a non-slave state, according to Massachusetts delegate Rufus King, but it was "a necessary sacrifice to the establishment of the Constitution."

Size of Congress

The convention committee that recommended equal representation in the Senate on July 5 also proposed that each state have one vote in the House for every 40,000 inhabitants. This proposal precipitated the debate on representation, during which it was decided to let Congress regulate the future size of the House to allow for population changes and the admission of new states. Upon reflection by the delegates, however, it was feared that under such an arrangement a majority in Congress would be able to block a reapportionment plan or change the basis of representation for slaves. Thus northerners and southerners now agreed that the periods between reapportionments and the rules for revising representation in the House ought to be fixed by the Constitution.

Edmund Randolph was the first to propose a regular census, and on July 13 the convention adopted the plan, finally incorporated in Article I, Section 2, linking the apportionment of representatives to an "enumeration" every 10 years of the "whole number of free persons . . . and three fifths of all others." On August 8 it was decided that the number of representatives "shall not exceed one for every 40,000," a figure that was lowered to 30,000 on the last day of the convention. Until the first census was taken, the size of the House was fixed at 65 representatives, allotted as set forth in Article I.

The size of the Senate was fixed on July 23 when the convention adopted a proposal (which Maryland alone voted against) that the body should "consist of two members from each state, who shall vote per capita." A proposal to allow each state three senators had been turned down on the ground that it would penalize poorer and more distant states and that "a small number was most convenient for deciding on peace and war," as Nathaniel Gorham put it.

The idea that senators should vote individually rather than as a delegation came from Elbridge Gerry, who wanted to "prevent the delays and inconveniences" that had occurred in Congress in voting under the unit rule. Although this provision was at odds with the decision that the states should be equally represented in the Senate, it was accepted with little objection and included in Article I, Section 3.

Terms of Office

There was strong attachment in the convention to the tradition of annual elections — "the only defense of the people against tyranny," according to Gerry. But Madison argued that representatives would need more than one year to become informed about the office and the national interests, and his proposal of a three-year term for the House was adopted June 12. Many delegates continued to press for more frequent elections, however. "The Representatives ought to return home and mix with the people," said Sherman, adding that "by remaining at the seat of Government they would acquire the habits of the place, which might differ from those of their constituents." The convention reconsidered the question June 21 and compromised on biennial elections and a two-year term for representatives.

The delegates also changed their minds about the Senate, agreeing first to a term of seven years, although the terms of state senators varied from two years to a maximum of five. When this decision was reviewed, alternatives of four, six and nine years were considered. Charles Pinckney opposed six years. Senators would be "too long separated from their constituents, and will imbibe attachments different from that of the state," he argued. But having decided on biennial elections for the House, the convention voted June 26 to make it a six-year term in the Senate, with one-third of the membership to be elected every two years.

Qualifications of Voters

The August 6 report of the convention's Committee of Detail stated that the qualifications of electors for the House should be the same as those required by the states for "the most numerous branch" of their own legislatures. Because property and other voting qualifications varied widely from state to state, no uniform standard seemed feasible. When Gouverneur Morris proposed giving Congress power to alter the qualifications, Oliver Ellsworth objected: "The clause is safe as it is — the states have staked their liberties on the qualifications which we have proposed to confirm." A proposal by Morris and others to limit the franchise to those who owned land was rejected, and on August 8 the convention adopted the committee's proposal without dissent.

Regulation of Elections

The Committee of Detail also proposed that the states regulate the times and places of electing senators and representatives, but that Congress retain the power to change these regulations. The states should not have the last word in this regard, said Madison, since "it was impossible to foresee all the abuses that might be made of the discretionary power." The convention adopted this provision on August 9 but amended it September 14 by adding the qualification: "except as to the places of choosing Senators," who were to be elected by the state legislatures. The purpose of the change was to "exempt the seats of government in the states from the power of Congress."

Qualifications of Members

The convention decided in June on a minimum age of 30 for senators and 25 for representatives. The Committee of Detail added two more qualifications: United States citizenship (three years for the House, four for the Senate) and residence within the state to be represented. Fearful of making it too easy for foreigners to be elected, the convention lengthened the citizenship requirement to seven years for representatives and nine years for senators, after voting down 14 years as likely, in Ellsworth's view, to discourage "meritorious aliens from emigrating to this country."

Some delegates wanted to require residence in a state for a minimum time — from one to seven years. Mason feared that "rich men of neighboring states may employ with success the means of corruption in some particular district and thereby get into the public councils after having failed in their own state." But these proposals were voted down, and it was left that "no person shall be a representative [or senator] who shall not, when elected, be an inhabitant of that state in which he shall be chosen."

The convention debated the desirability of a property qualification for office. Most of the state constitutions required members of their legislatures to own certain amounts of property. John Dickinson doubted the wisdom of a "policy of interweaving into a Republican Constitution a veneration of wealth." But on July 26, by a vote of eight states to three, the convention instructed the Committee of Detail to draft a property qualification. As written, this would have given Congress authority to establish "uniform qualifications ... with regard to property." When the provision was debated on August 10 it was rejected, and further efforts to include a property qualification ended.

There was even less disposition to include a religious qualification, although all of the states except New York and Virginia imposed such a qualification on state representatives. The convention's outlook on this point was made clear when, in debating an oath of office on August 30, the delegates adopted without dissent Charles Pinckney's proviso (which became a part of Article VI) that "no religious test shall ever be required as a qualification to any office or public trust under the United States." Thus the only qualifications established by the Constitution for election to Congress were those of age, citizenship and residence.

Pay of Members

The Virginia Plan wanted members of the National Legislature to be paid "liberal stipends" without saying who should pay them. To the nationalists, however, one of the weaknesses of the Confederation was that members of Congress were paid by their states. So on June 12, after submitting "fixt" for "liberal," the Committee of the Whole agreed that in the case of representatives "the wages should be paid out of the National Treasury." Ellsworth dissented and on June 22 moved that the states pay their salaries. This change was opposed by Randolph who said it would create a dependence that "would vitiate the whole system." Hamilton agreed: "[T]hose who pay are the masters of those who are paid." Ellsworth's motion was rejected, four states to five.

When the pay of senators was discussed on June 26, Ellsworth again moved that the states pay. Madison argued that this would make senators "the mere agents and advocates of state interests and views, instead of being the impartial umpires and guardians of justice and general good." Ellsworth's motion was again defeated, five states to six. Despite the vote, the August 6 report of the Committee of Detail provided that the pay of senators and representatives should be "ascertained and paid" by the states. But Ellsworth and others by now had changed their minds, and on August 14 the convention voted nine states to two to pay members out of the national Treasury.

Whether the amount of pay should be fixed in the Constitution was another matter. To let Congress set its own wages, said Madison, "was an indecent thing and might, in time, prove a dangerous one." Ellsworth proposed five dollars a day. Others thought the decision should be left to Congress, although Sherman was afraid the members would pay themselves too little rather than too much, "so that men ever so fit could not serve unless they were at the same time rich." On August 14 the convention voted to give Congress full authority to fix its own pay by law.

Length of Service

Because of the attachment of several states to the theory of rotation in office, the Articles of Confederation had provided that "no person shall be capable of being a delegate for more than three years in any term of six years." This rule had forced out of Congress some of its better members and was widely criticized. The Virginia Plan proposed, nevertheless, that members ought not to be eligible for re-election indefinitely after the expiration of their initial term of service, and that they should be subject to recall. But this provision was eliminated in the Committee of the Whole, without debate or dissent, and no further effort was made to restrict the eligibility of representatives or senators for re-election.

Whether members of Congress should be eligible to hold other offices was more controversial. Under the Articles, a delegate was not "capable of holding any office under the United States for which he, or another for his benefit, receives any salary, fees or emolument of any kind." The Congress had appointed many delegates to diplomatic and other jobs, however, and the practice had created much resentment.

The office seeking propensities of state legislators also raised general concern. The Virginia Plan proposed making any member of Congress ineligible for any office established by a particular state, or under the authority of the United States, during this term of service and for an unspecified period after its expiration.

Although this provision, with a period of one year inserted in the blank, was adopted in the Committee of the Whole on June 12, the convention reconsidered and modified it several times before the final form was approved on September 3. Delegates who wanted to shut the door on appointments saw them as a source of corruption. "What led to the appointment of this Convention?" asked John Mercer, who answered: "The corruption and mutability of the legislative councils of the states." Those opposed to too many strictures feared they would discourage good men from running for Congress. "The legislature would cease to be a magnet to the first talents and abilities," said Charles Pinckney.

The compromise that emerged was a twofold disqualification. First, a member could not be appointed during his term to a federal office created during his term or to a federal office for which the pay was increased during the member's term. Second, no one holding federal office could be a member of Congress at the same time. The provision, incorporated in Section 6 of Article I, made no reference to state office or to ineligibility following expiration of a member's term.

Rules and Regulation of Congress

Article I included four provisions for the regulation of the House and Senate that originated with the Committee of Detail and were modified only slightly by the full convention:

— "Each House shall be the Judge of the Elections, Returns and Qualifications of its own Members. . . ." The constitutions of eight of the states contained this language, and it was agreed to without debate.

— "Each House may determine the Rules of its Proceedings, punish its Members for disorderly Behaviour, and, with the Concurrence of two-thirds, expel a Member." This provision was amended by the two-thirds vote requirement for expulsion. The change, proposed by Madison because "the right of expulsion was too important to be exercised by a bare majority of a quorum," was approved unanimously.

— "Each House shall keep a Journal, and from time to time publish the same. . . ." This language stemmed from a similar provision in the Articles of Confederation. When Madison proposed giving the Senate some discretion in the matter, Wilson objected: "[T]he people have a right to know what their agents are doing or have done, and it should not be in the option of the legislature to conceal their proceedings." The convention voted to require publication of the Journals of each House, "excepting such parts as may in their judgment require secrecy." The clause also provided for recording the "yea" and "nay" votes of members, although some delegates objected that "the reasons governing the votes never appear along with them."

— "Neither House, during the Session of Congress, shall, without the Consent of the other, adjourn for more than three days, nor to any other Place than that in which the two Houses shall be sitting." This was agreed to after brief debate. Most of the state constitutions had similar provisions, reflecting a common reaction against the practice of royal governors to suspend and dissolve the state assemblies.

POWERS OF CONGRESS

The resolutions introduced May 29 by Edmund Randolph of Virginia reflected the great concern of the nationalists with the powerlessness of Congress under the Articles of Confederation to protect the interests of the United States at large. James Dickinson warned against the "prejudices, passions and improper views of the state legislatures," and James Madison deplored "a constant tendency in the states to encroach on the federal authority, to violate national treaties, to infringe the rights and interests of each other, to oppress the weaker party within their respective jurisdiction." Delegates at the Constitutional Convention of 1787 felt it was essential that, in addition to adequate authority to legislate for the general interests of the Union, the new national government should possess the power to restrain the states and to compel their obedience.

The Virginia resolutions proposed that the National Legislature be empowered:

"to enjoy the Legislative Rights vested in Congress by the Confederation and moreover to legislate in all cases to which the separate States are incompetent, or in which the harmony of the United States may be interrupted by the exercise of individual Legislation;

"to negate all laws passed by the several States, contravening in the opinion of the National Legislature the articles of Union; and

"to call forth the force of the Union against any member of the Union failing in its duty under the articles thereof."

When these proposals were first discussed May 31, some delegates wanted an exact enumeration of such powers before voting, but the first of the Virginia resolutions was approved after brief debate without dissent. The second, granting a power to negate state laws — which was akin to the royal disallowance of colonial laws — also was approved easily. When the third resolution was called up, however, Madison moved to set it aside because he feared that "the use of force against a state would look more like a declaration of war than an infliction of punishment." Although the New Jersey Plan contained a similar provision, there was no further consideration of this power by the convention.

On June 8 Charles Pinckney proposed that the power to nullify state laws be extended to all such laws Congress should judge to be improper. Such an expansion would enslave the states, Elbridge Gerry argued, and the motion was rejected, seven states to three. Strong opposition then developed to any power to negate state laws, although Madison continued to defend it as the most certain means of preserving the system. On July 17 the convention reversed its earlier action by voting seven states to three against the power to veto. The problem of securing conformity of the states to national law finally was resolved by adoption of a "supremacy" clause and a specific prohibition on certain types of state laws.

The convention on July 17 also reconsidered the first of the Virginia resolutions. Roger Sherman proposed as a substitute that Congress be empowered "to make laws binding on the people of the United States in all cases which may concern the common interests of the Union; but not to interfere with the Government of the individual States in any matters of internal police which respect the Government of such States only, and wherein the general welfare of the United

States is not concerned." This formulation, in which the term "general welfare" made its first appearance in the convention, seemed too restrictive to most delegates; it was rejected, eight states to two. Then, by a vote of six states to four, the convention inserted in the resolution approved May 31 the additional power to legislate "in all cases for the general interests of the Union."

The Committee of Detail found this broad grant of legislative authority too vague and unlimited and decided to replace it with an enumeration of specified powers. Eighteen of these powers were listed in the committee's August 6 report, which also spelled out certain powers to be denied to Congress and to the states. These powers and prohibitions were finally incorporated in Sections 8, 9 and 10 of Article I of the Constitution.

Power to Tax

The committee's first proposal — that Congress "shall have the power to lay and collect taxes, duties, imposts and excises" — was adopted August 16 without dissent. The convention then became embroiled in the issue of paying off the public debt and decided to amend the tax clause to provide that Congress "shall fulfill the engagements and discharge the debts of the United States and shall have the power to lay and collect taxes. . . ." Pierce Butler objected that this language would require Congress to redeem at face value all government paper, including that held by "bloodsuckers who had speculated on the distresses of others and bought up securities at heavy discounts." He thought Congress should be free to buy up such holdings at less than full value.

As a result, the convention dropped the language added to the tax clause and adopted in its place the declaration found in Article VI: "All debts contracted and engagements entered into before the adoption of this Constitution shall be as valid against the United States under this Constitution as under the Confederation." (The question of full or partial redemption, which was to become a major issue in the First Congress, was left unresolved.) Some delegates then argued that the power to tax should be linked explicitly to the purpose of paying the debt. Their position led to further amendment of the tax clause on September 4 to provide that Congress "shall have power to lay and collect taxes, duties, imposts and excises, to pay the debts and provide for the common defense and general welfare of the United States."

It was to be argued later that inclusion of the words "general welfare" was intended to confer an additional and unlimited power on

Congress. The records of the convention indicate, however, that when it was decided to qualify the power to tax by adding the words "to pay the debts," it became necessary to make it clear that this was not the only purpose for which taxes could be levied. "To provide for the common defense and general welfare" was taken from the Articles of Confederation and used to encompass all of the other specific and limited powers vested by the Constitution in Congress.

In settling the basis for representation in the House, the convention had linked the apportionment of "direct taxes" as well as representatives to a count of all whites and three-fifths of the blacks. When this provision was reconsidered August 20, Rufus King asked, "What was the precise meaning of direct taxation?" According to Madison "no one answered." The only direct taxes in use at that time were land and capitation or poll taxes. Because southerners feared that Congress might seek to levy a special tax on slaves, the Committee of Detail recommended and the convention later adopted a further provision: "No Capitation, or other direct, Tax shall be laid, unless in Proportion" to the count required by Section 2. Another concession to the South incorporated in Section 9 of Article I was a prohibition of levies on exports.

Power to Regulate Commerce

A lack of uniformity in duties and commercial regulations under the Articles of Confederation severely handicapped trade among the states and with other countries. To Madison and many others, it was as essential to the new plan of government that Congress have the power to regulate commerce as it was that it have the power to tax. It soon became clear, however, that the southern states would not accept a Constitution that failed to protect their vested interest in slave labor and agricultural exports from the burdensome restrictions that a Congress controlled by northerners might seek to impose.

As a result, the Committee of Detail proposed that Congress be given the power to regulate commerce with foreign nations and among the several states, subject to two limitations: a ban on taxing exports and a prohibition on efforts to tax or outlaw the slave trade. The general power to regulate commerce was approved on August 16 without dissent. (The words "and with the Indian Tribes" were added September 4.) The proposed limitations met with considerable opposition, however.

In keeping with mercantilist doctrines, it was common practice at that time for governments to tax exports. The idea of prohibiting such action was novel. "To deny this power is to take from the common government half the regulation of trade," argued James Wilson of Philadelphia. It also would deny Congress the power to menace the livelihood of the South by taxing exports of rice, tobacco and indigo on which its economy was largely dependent. Some northerners, however, considered this concession to the South as wise as it was necessary. Massachusetts delegate Gerry said the convention already had given Congress "more power than we know how will be exercised." On August 21, by a vote of seven states to four, the convention agreed that "No Tax or Duty shall be laid on Articles exported from any State." This provision was placed in Section 9 of Article I in the final draft.

The second limitation on the power to regulate commerce provided that no tax or duty was to be laid on the migration or importation of such persons as the several States shall think proper to admit; nor shall such migration or importation be prohibited. The limitation was designed to meet the South's objection to any interference with the slave trade, although those words were carefully avoided. Luther Martin thought it was "inconsistent with the principles of the Revolution and dishonorable to the American character to have such a feature in the Constitution." But most other delegates, including those opposed to slavery, argued that it was a political rather than a moral issue.

Some northerners as well as southerners agreed with Oliver Ellsworth of Connecticut that "the morality or wisdom of slavery" should be left to the states to determine. "Let us not intermeddle," he said, predicting that "slavery, in time will not be a speck in our country." Many others agreed with George Mason that the "infernal traffic" in slaves was holding back the economic development of the country and that for this reason the national government "should have power to prevent the increase of slavery." Since the provision reported by the Committee of Detail was clearly unacceptable to many delegates, a committee was named to seek a compromise.

The panel now proposed that Congress be barred from prohibiting the slave trade until the year 1800, but that it have power to levy a duty on slaves as on other imports. Both provisions were approved August 25, the first by a vote of seven states to four (after the year 1800 had been changed to 1808), and the second after limiting the duty to $10 per person. These provisions concerning slaves, incorporated in the first clause of Section 9 of Article I, further limited Congress's power to regulate commerce.

Still another limit on the commerce power sought by the South and recommended by the Committee of Detail would have required a two-thirds vote of both houses of Congress to pass a navigation act. England had used such laws to channel colonial imports and exports into British ships and ports, and southerners now feared that the North, where shipping was a major interest, might try to monopolize the transport of their exports by a law requiring them to be carried aboard American ships.

Northern delegates were strongly opposed to the two-thirds proposal, and in working out the compromise on the slave trade they succeeded in having it dropped. As a result, Pinckney moved to require a two-thirds vote of both houses to enact any commercial regulation. This motion was rejected August 29 by seven states to four, and the convention confirmed the decision to drop the proposed two-thirds rule for navigation acts. Mason, one of three delegates who refused to sign the Constitution, later argued that a bare majority of Congress should not have the power to "enable a few rich merchants in Philadelphia, New York and Boston to monopolize the staples of the Southern States."

A relatively minor limitation on the power to regulate commerce was adopted to allay the fear of Maryland that Congress might require ships traversing the Chesapeake Bay to enter or clear at Norfolk or another Virginia port in order to simplify the collection of duties. As approved August 31 and added to Section 9, Article I, the added language provided that "No Preference shall be given by any Regulation of Commerce or Revenue to the Ports of one State over those of another; nor shall Vessels bound to or from one State be obliged to enter, clear or pay Duties in another."

War and Treaty Power

The Articles of Confederation had given Congress the exclusive right and power of deciding issues of peace and war. The Committee of Detail proposed giving to the new Congress as a whole the power to make war and giving to the Senate alone the power to approve treaties. Subsequently, the treaty power was divided between the president and the Senate, but in discussing the war-making power on August 17, Pinckney favored giving that authority exclusively to the Senate. "It would be singular for one authority to make war, and another peace," he reasoned. Butler, on the other hand, felt the war power should rest with the president, "who will have all the requisite qualities and will not make war but when the Nation will support it." Neither view drew any support, and the convention voted to give Congress the power "to declare war." The word "declare" had been substituted for "make" in order to leave the president free to repel a sudden attack. Sherman said, "The Executive should be able to repel, and not commence, war."

On August 18 the convention agreed to give Congress the power "to raise and support Armies," "to provide and maintain a Navy," and "to make Rules for the Government and Regulation of the land and naval Forces." All of these provisions were taken from the Articles of Confederation. Gerry, voicing the old colonial fears of a standing army, wanted a proviso that "in time of peace" the army should consist of no more than two or three thousand men, but his motion was unanimously rejected. On September 5, however, the convention added to the power to "raise and support Armies" the proviso that "no Appropriation of Money to that Use shall be for a longer Term than two Years." This was intended to quiet fears similar to those that had led the British to require annual appropriations for the army.

The convention approved without dissent the power, proposed by the Committee of Detail and included in Section 8, Article I, "to provide for calling forth the Militia to execute the Laws of the Union, suppress Insurrections and repel Invasions." But a further proposal by Mason that Congress have the power to regulate the militia alarmed the defenders of state sovereignty. To Gerry this was the last point remaining to be surrendered. Others argued that the states would never allow control of the militia to get out of their hands.

The shortcomings of the militia during the Revolutionary War were a bitter memory to most of the delegates, however, and they shared the practical view of Madison that "as the greatest danger to liberty is from large standing armies, it is best to prevent them by an effectual provision for a good militia." So on August 23 the convention adopted the provision, as later incorporated in Section 8, giving Congress power "to provide for organizing, arming, and disciplining the Militia, and for governing such Part of them as may be employed in the Service of the United States. . . ."

Special Status of Money Bills

The committee named to resolve the issue of equal or proportional representation in the Senate had proposed as a compromise that each state have one vote in the Senate, but that the House originate all bills to raise and appropriate money or pay government salaries and that the Senate be denied the right to amend such bills. Included in the proposal was the phrase, "No money shall be drawn from the public Treasury, but in pursuance of appropriations to be originated in the first branch." Seven states at this time required that money bills originate in the lower house, but only four of those states forbade amendment by the upper house. Although some delegates objected that such a provision would be degrading to the Senate, it was approved July 6 by a vote of five states to three.

The Committee of Detail phrased the provision as follows: "All bills for raising or appropriating money, and for fixing the salaries of the officers of Government, shall originate in the House of Representatives, and shall not be altered or amended by the Senate." Madison feared the provision would promote "injurious altercations" between House and Senate; others insisted that it was necessary because the people "will not agree that any but their immediate representatives shall meddle with their purse." The convention's division on the question reflected contrasting concepts of the Senate as likely to be the most responsible branch or the most aristocratic one, to be strengthened or checked accordingly.

But on August 8 the convention reversed itself and dropped the provision. A compromise adopted September 8 by a vote of nine states to two provided that "All bills for raising revenue shall originate in the House of Representatives, and shall be subject to alterations and amendments by the Senate; no money shall be drawn from the Treasury but in consequence of appropriations made by law." The first clause, slightly revised, was incorporated in Section 7, while the second clause was made one of the limitations on the powers of Congress listed in Section 9, Article I.

The Constitution thus gave the House exclusive power to originate any bill involving taxes or tariffs, but it did not extend that power to include appropriations bills. However, the House assumed that additional power on the basis of the consideration it had received in the convention; it became the recognized prerogative of the House to originate spending as well as revenue bills.

Admission of New States

As early as 1780 the Continental Congress had resolved that lands ceded to the United States "shall be disposed of for the common benefit of the United States, and be settled and formed into distinct republican States, which shall become members of the Federal Union, and have the same rights of sovereignty, freedom and independence as the other States." By 1786 the Congress of the Confederation was in possession of all land south of Canada, north of the Ohio, west of the Allegheny Mountains and east of the Mississippi. Guidelines for governing this great territory were laid down by Congress in the Northwest Ordinance of July 13, 1787.

The Ordinance provided that, upon attaining a population of 5,000 free male inhabitants of voting age, the territory would be entitled to elect a legislature and send a nonvoting delegate to Congress. No less than three or more than five states were to be formed out of the territory. Each state was to have at least 60,000 free inhabitants to qualify for admission to the Union "on an equal footing with the original States in all respects whatever." And the Ordinance declared that "there shall be neither slavery nor involuntary servitude in the said territory. . . ."

At the same time as this farsighted plan was being approved in New York by the Congress of the Confederation, Gouverneur Morris and other eastern delegates to the Constitutional Convention in Philadelphia were arguing strongly against equality for the new states. Numerous objections were raised. "The busy haunts of men, not the remote wilderness, are the proper school of political talents," said Morris. "If the western people get the power into their hands, they will ruin the Atlantic interests. The back members are always most adverse to the best measures."

Among those opposing this view were the delegates of Virginia and North Carolina, whose western lands were to become Kentucky and Tennessee. Mason argued that the western territories "will either not unite with or will speedily revolt from the Union, if they are not in all respects placed on an equal footing." In time, he thought they might well be "both more numerous and more wealthy" than the seaboard states. Madison was certain that "no unfavorable distinctions were admissible, either in point of justice or policy."

In the light of that debate, the Committee of Detail proposed on August 6 that Congress have the power to admit new states upon the consent of two-thirds of the members present of each house and, in the case of a state formed from an existing state, upon the consent of the legislature of that state. New states were to be admitted on the same terms as the original states. But when this proposal was considered August 29, the convention adopted a motion by Morris to drop the provision for equality of admission.

Morris and Dickinson then offered a new draft, eliminating the condition of a two-thirds vote in favor of a simple majority, which was adopted and became the first clause of Section 3, Article IV. It provided simply that new states could be admitted by Congress. Although this provision of the Constitution was silent as to the status of the new states, Congress was to adhere to the principle of equality in admitting them.

The convention then adopted the provision governing territories set out in the second clause of Section 3, Article IV. Madison had first proposed adding such a provision to the Constitution to give a legal foundation to the Northwest Ordinance, since the Articles of Confederation had given Congress no explicit power to legislate for territories. A proviso ruling out prejudice to any claims of the United States or of a particular state was added because some delegates feared that, without it, the terms on which new states were admitted might favor the claims of a state to vacant lands ceded by Britain.

Power of Impeachment

It was decided early in the convention that the chief executive should be "removable on impeachment and conviction of malpractice or neglect of duty." Who should impeach and try him, however, depended on how he was to be chosen. So long as Congress was to elect the president — and that decision stood until September 4 — few delegates were willing to give Congress the additional power to remove him. The final decision to have the president chosen by presidential electors helped to resolve the problem.

The Virginia Plan called for the national judiciary to try "impeachments of any National officers," without specifying which branch of government would impeach. Because all the state constitutions vested that power in the lower house of the assembly, the Committee of Detail proposed removal of the president on impeachment by the House and conviction by the Supreme Court "of treason, bribery or corruption." No action was taken on this proposal until the special committee, in advancing the plan for presidential electors, suggested that the Senate try all impeachments and that conviction require the concurrence of two-thirds of the members present.

When this plan was debated September 8, Pinckney opposed trial by the Senate on the ground that if the president "opposes a favorite law, the two Houses will combine against him, and under the influence of heat and faction throw him out of office." Nevertheless, the convention adopted the formula for impeachment by the House, trial by the Senate, and conviction by a two-thirds vote. It also extended the grounds for impeachment from treason and bribery to "other high crimes and other misdemeanors" and made the vice president and other civil officers similarly impeachable and removable. These provisions were incorporated in Sections 2 and 3 of Article I and in Section 4 of Article II.

Miscellaneous Powers

The Committee of Detail proposed that Congress retain the power granted in the Articles "to borrow money and emit bills on the credit of the United States." But state emissions of paper money in 1786 had contributed greatly to the alarms that had led to the calling of the convention, and most delegates agreed with Ellsworth that this was a "favorable moment to shut and bar the door against paper money." So the words "and emit bills" were struck when this provision was approved August 16.

Most of the other powers of Congress specified in Section 8 of Article I — concerning naturalization and bankruptcy, coinage, counterfeiting, post offices, copyrights, inferior tribunals, piracies and the seat of government — were approved with little debate. The final provision of Section 8, one of the most sweeping grants of power in the entire Constitution, also attracted little attention at the time. That clause authorized Congress "to make all Laws which shall be necessary and proper for carrying into Execution the foregoing Powers, and all other Powers vested by this Constitution in the Government of the United States, or in any Department or Officer thereof." The intent of this grant was simply to enable Congress to enact legislation giving effect to the specified powers. No member of the convention suggested that it conferred powers in addition to those previously specified in the article. But the meaning of the clause and of the words "necessary and proper" was to become the focus of the controversy between broad and strict constructionists of the Constitution that began with the passage by the First Congress of a law creating a national bank.

Limits on Congressional Power

Section 9 of Article I imposed eight specific limitations on the powers of Congress. Those relating to the slave trade, capitation taxes, sport taxes, preference among ports and appropriations have been discussed in connection with the powers to tax, regulate commerce and originate money bills. The other three were adopted as follows:

— On August 28 Pinckney moved to adopt a provision in the Massachusetts Constitution that barred suspension of the writ of habeas corpus except on the most urgent occasions and then for a period not to exceed one year. This was amended and adopted to provide that "the Privilege of the Writ of Habeas Corpus shall not be suspended, unless when in Cases of Rebellion or Invasion the public Safety may require it."

— On August 22 Gerry proposed a prohibition on the passage of bills of attainder and ex post facto laws. Some delegates objected that such a provision would imply an improper suspicion of Congress and that it was unnecessary. The convention agreed, however, that "No Bill of Attainder or ex post facto Law shall be passed." A subsequent motion by Mason, to delete ex post facto laws on the ground that the ban might prevent Congress from redeeming the war debt at less than face value, was rejected unanimously.

— On August 23 the convention adopted the two provisions that make up the final clause of Section 9, Article I, both of which were taken from the Articles of Confederation. The bar to titles of nobility was proposed by the Committee of Detail. The bar to acceptance of emolument, office or title from foreign governments without the consent of Congress was urged by Pinckney to help keep American officials independent of external influence.

Pinckney and others proposed adding to the Constitution a number of provisions similar to those contained in the Bills of Rights of the various states. On September 12 Gerry moved to appoint a committee to draft a Bill of Rights, but 10 states voted no. Anxious to complete their work and return home, the delegates were in no mood to spend more time on something most of them believed to be unnecessary since none of the powers to be vested in Congress seemed to countenance legislation that might violate individual rights.

The omission of a Bill of Rights later became a major issue in seeking the states' approval of the Constitution and led to assurances by those favoring ratification that guarantees would be added to the Constitution promptly once the new system of government was established.

THE EXECUTIVE BRANCH

No question troubled the convention more than the powers and structure to be given the executive in the new government. The office did not exist under the Articles of Confederation, which placed the executive function in Congress. A longstanding fear of executive authority had led Americans "to throw all power into the Legislative vortex," as James Madison explained it. Under most of the state constitutions, the executives were indeed "little more than cyphers, the

Legislatures omnipotent." How much more authority and independence to give the national executive remained in dispute until the very end of the convention.

The Virginia Plan had recommended a national executive chosen by the legislative branch for a fixed term. He would be ineligible for reappointment and empowered with "a general authority to execute the National laws" as well as "the Executive rights vested in Congress by the Confederation." Debate on these proposals disclosed a spectrum of views. Many delegates were wary of a return of executive authority such as that exercised by the royal governor's or by the King. Roger Sherman thought the executive should be "nothing more than an institution for carrying the will of the Legislature into effect." Gouverneur Morris, on the other hand, believed the executive should be "the firm guardian of the people" against legislative tyranny.

Until September, the last month of the convention, most delegates favored a single executive, chosen by Congress for a single term of seven years, whose authority would be limited by the power of Congress to appoint judges and ambassadors and make treaties. This plan for legislative supremacy was then abandoned for the more balanced one that finally was adopted and incorporated in Article II of the Constitution. A president would be chosen by electors for a four-year term without limit as to re-election, and he would have the power to make all appointments subject to confirmation by the Senate and to make treaties subject to approval by a two-thirds vote of the Senate.

A Single Executive

Edmund Randolph, who presented the Virginia Plan, opposed a single executive as "the foetus of monarchy" and proposed three persons, who, George Mason thought, should be chosen from the northern, middle and southern states. But James Wilson foresaw "nothing but uncontrolled, continued and violent animosities" among three persons. A single executive, he said, would give "most energy, dispatch and responsibility to the office." On June 4 the delegates voted for a single executive, seven states to four, and the convention confirmed the decision July 17 without dissent.

The Committee of Detail then proposed that "the Executive Power of the United States shall be vested in a single person" to be called the president and to have the title of "His Excellency." These provisions were adopted August 24 without debate, but in drafting the final document the Committee of Style dropped the title and provided simply that "the Executive Power shall be vested in a President of the

United States of America." The omission from the Constitution of any title other than president helped to defeat a proposal in the First Congress that he be addressed as "His Highness."

Method of Election, Term of Office

The method of election and the term of office of the executive were closely related issues. If Congress were to choose the president, most delegates thought he should have a fairly long term and be ineligible for reappointment. For as Randolph put it, "if he should be reappointable by the Legislature, he will be no check on it." But if the president was to be chosen in some other manner, a shorter term with re-eligibility was favored by most of the delegates. Thus the method of election was the key question.

The convention first decided that Congress should choose the president for a single seven-year term. On reflection, however, some delegates thought this would not leave him sufficiently independent. Wilson proposed election by electors chosen by the people, but Elbridge Gerry considered the people "too little informed of personal characters" to choose electors, and the proposal was rejected, eight to two. Gerry proposed that the governors of the states pick the president to avoid the corruption he foresaw in having Congress choose, but this plan also was scratched.

Several other methods were proposed, and at one point the delegates agreed on selection by electors chosen by the state legislatures. But this decision then was reversed. However, when Gouverneur Morris on August 24 renewed Wilson's original proposal for electors chosen by the people only six states were opposed; five voted in favor of it. Three of the latter were smaller states that had opposed an earlier proposal to have the membership of the Senate and the House vote to elect the president, thereby giving the large states (having a greater number of representatives) a bigger voice in the decision.

All of the questions concerning the presidency then were reconsidered by the Special Committee on Postponed Matters, whose report of September 4 recommended most of the provisions that were finally adopted. According to Morris, the committee rejected the choosing of the president by Congress because of "the danger of intrigue and faction" and "the opportunity for cabal." Instead, it proposed that he be chosen by electors equal in number to the senators and representatives from each state, who would be chosen as each state decided. They would vote by ballot for two persons, at least one of whom could not be an inhabitant of their state. The one receiving a majority of the

The President's Cabinet

In 1787 eight states had a Privy Council to advise the governor, and the idea of providing for a similar body to advise the president was discussed at length at the Constitutional Convention. Elbridge Gerry thought it would "give weight and inspire confidence" in the executive. Benjamin Franklin concurred: "A Council would not only be a check on a bad President, but be a relief to a good one." But Gouverneur Morris disagreed: "Give him an able Council and it will thwart him; a weak one, and he will shelter himself under their sanction." *

On August 22 the Committee of Detail submitted to the convention the following proposal, first offered by Morris and Charles Pinckney:

*The President of the United States shall have a Privy Council which shall consist of the President of the Senate, the Speaker of the House of Representatives, the Chief Justice of the Supreme Court, and the principal officer in the respective departments of Foreign Affairs, Domestic Affairs, War, Marine, and Finance, as such departments of office shall from time to time be established, whose duty it shall be to advise him in matters respecting the execution of his office, which he shall think proper to lay before them; but their advice shall not conclude him, nor affect his responsibility for the measures which he shall adopt.***

The convention did not vote on this proposal. The September 4 report of the Special Committee on Postponed Matters proposed only that the president "may require the Opinion in writing of the principal Officer in each of the executive Departments, upon any Subject relating to the Duties of their respective Offices." This provision — adopted September 7 after the convention had rejected the idea of an executive council to be appointed by Congress — was included among the powers of the president set out in Article II, Section 2.

The word "Cabinet" was not used in the convention or in the Constitution. But as that body developed under Washington and later presidents, it conformed to the limited role that had been envisioned in the Morris-Pinckney proposal for a Privy Council.

* Charles Warren, *The Making of the Constitution* (Boston: Little, Brown & Co., 1928), p. 646.
** Ibid., pp. 646-47.

electoral votes would become president, the one with the next largest vote would become vice president. In the event of a tie, or if no one received a majority, the Senate would decide.

The plan provided for a four-year term with no restriction as to re-election; shifted from the Senate to the president the power to appoint ambassadors and judges and to make treaties subject to Senate approval; and gave to the Senate, instead of the Supreme Court, the power to try impeachments. This realignment of powers between the president and the Senate appealed to the small states because it was generally assumed that the Senate (in which each state was to be represented equally) would have the final say in choosing the president in most cases.

For the same reason, however, some delegates now feared that the combination of powers to be vested in the Senate would, in Randolph's words, "convert that body into a real and dangerous aristocracy." Sherman thereupon proposed moving the final election of the president from the Senate to the House, with the proviso that each state have one vote. The change, which preserved the influence of the small states while easing the fears expressed about the Senate, was quickly adopted, as was the rest of the electoral plan and the four-year term without limit as to re-eligibility.

Qualifications

The Committee of Detail first proposed that a president be at least 35 years of age, a citizen and an inhabitant of the United States for 21 years, just as age, citizenship and minimum period of residence were the only qualifications stipulated for senators and representatives. The committee added the qualification that the president had to be a natural-born citizen or a citizen at the time of the adoption of the Constitution, and it reduced the time of residence within the United States to at least 14 years "in the whole." The phrase "in the whole" was dropped in drafting the final provision of Section 1, Article II, which also was adjusted to make it clear that the qualifications for president applied equally to the vice president.

The Vice President

The office of the vice president was not considered by the convention until September 4, when the Special Committee on Postponed Matters proposed that a vice president, chosen for the same term as the president, serve as ex officio president of the Senate. (A vice president or lieutenant governor served in a similar capacity in four of the

13 states.) The proposal was designed to provide a position for the runner-up in the electoral vote and to give the Senate an impartial presiding officer without depriving any state of one of its two votes.

When this proposal was debated September 7, Mason objected that "it mixed too much the Legislative and the Executive." Gerry thought it tantamount to putting the president himself at the head of the Senate because of "the close intimacy that must subsist between the president and the vice president." But Sherman noted that "if the Vice President were not to be President of the Senate, he would be without employment." The convention adopted the proposal of the special committee, with only Massachusetts opposed. The provision that the vice president "shall be president of the Senate, but shall have no Vote unless they be equally divided," was placed in Section 3 of Article I.

In case of the president's impeachment, death, absence, resignation or inability to discharge the powers or duties of his office, the special committee proposed that "the Vice President shall exercise those powers and duties until another President be chosen, or until the inability of the President be removed." This language was revised slightly in Article II, Section 1: "In case of the removal of the President from office, or of his death, resignation, or inability to discharge the powers and duties of the said office, the same shall devolve on the Vice President." The revised wording left it unclear whether the "said office" or the "powers and duties" were to "devolve" on the vice president. The right of the vice president to assume the office of president was first asserted by John Tyler in 1841. He assumed the presidency on the death of William Henry Harrison and served for the remainder of Harrison's term, thus establishing the practice.

There remained the question of providing for the office in the event both men died or were removed. Randolph proposed that Congress designate an officer to "act accordingly until the time of electing a President shall arrive." Madison objected that this would prevent an earlier election, so it was agreed to substitute "until such disability be removed, or a President shall be elected." The Committee of Style ignored this change, so the convention voted on September 15 to restore it. The final provision, authorizing Congress to designate by law an officer to "act as President" until "a President shall be elected," was joined to the earlier provision in Article II that related to the vice president.

Presidential Powers

Initially, the convention conferred only three powers on the president: "to carry into effect the National laws," "to appoint to offices in cases not otherwise provided for," and to veto bills. The Committee of Detail proposed a number of additional powers drawn from the state constitutions, most of which were adopted with little discussion or change. This was true of provisions placed in Section 3 of Article II for informing Congress "of the State of the Union" and recommending legislation to convene and adjourn Congress, receive ambassadors, and see "that the Laws be faithfully executed."

The convention also agreed without debate that "the President shall be Commander in Chief of the Army and Navy" and of the militia when called into national service. Almost all of the state constitutions vested a similar power in the state executives. The power of the president "to grant reprieves and pardons except in cases of impeachment" likewise was approved, although Mason argued that Congress should have this power and Randolph wanted to bar pardons for treason as "too great a trust" to place in the president. These two provisions were included in Section 2 of Article II.

Power to Appoint. The appointive powers of the president initially were limited by the convention to "cases not otherwise provided for." The Virginia Plan had proposed that judges be appointed by the national legislature, a practice followed in all except three states, but the delegates voted to give the power to the Senate alone as the "less numerous and more select body." In July the delegates considered and rejected alternative proposals that judges be appointed by the president alone, by the president with the advice and consent of the Senate, and by the president unless two-thirds of the Senate disagreed.

By late summer, sentiment had changed. On September 7 the convention adopted the proposal of the special committee that the president appoint ambassadors and other public ministers, justices of the Supreme Court and all other officers of the United States "by and with the Advice and Consent of the Senate." This power, incorporated in Section 2, later was qualified by requiring that offices not otherwise provided for "be established by law" and by authorizing Congress to vest appointment of lower level officers in the presidency, the courts and the heads of departments. Nothing was said about a presidential power to remove executive branch officials from office once confirmed by the Senate — a power that was to become a much-argued issue.

Two-Thirds Majority Rule

To the men who drafted the Constitution, a major weakness of the Articles of Confederation was the rule that nine (or two-thirds) of the 13 states had to concur in all important decisions. Therefore, they specified that in the two chambers of Congress "a Majority of each shall constitute a Quorum to do Business." (Article I, Section 5) With respect to certain powers, however, the delegates decided to require more than a simple majority vote:

— For conviction through impeachment by the Senate, which requires the concurrence of two-thirds of senators present and voting.

— Approval of treaties with other countries, which requires the concurrence of two-thirds of senators present and voting.

— Expelling a member of Congress, which requires a two-thirds vote of the House or Senate, respectively.

— Enacting a bill over the president's veto, which requires a two-thirds vote of both houses.

— Proposed constitutional amendments, which require a two-thirds vote of both houses before they can be submitted to the states for ratification.

— Selection of the president by the House — the constitutional requirement when no candidate receives a majority of the electoral votes — requiring the presence of a quorum, which must "consist of a Member or Members from two-thirds of the States. . . ." (Once a quorum is established, however, a simple majority is sufficient to elect the president, with each state delegation in the House allowed to cast one vote.)

Of the provisions included in the Constitution, only those relating to the Senate's role in trying impeachments and approving treaties made it clear that the decision rested with two-thirds of the members present and voting, rather than with two-thirds of the entire membership. There is persuasive evidence that the latter interpretation was intended by the delegates for the provisions relating to vetoes, expulsion of members and constitutional amendments. However, in the absence of an explicit requirement to that effect, Congress over the years had established the precedent that two-thirds of members "present" and voting likewise was sufficient for a decision in those cases — an assumption sustained by the Supreme Court in 1919 *(Missouri Pac. R.R. Co. v. Kansas)* and 1920 *(Rhode Island v. Palmer)*.

Treaty Power. The Committee of Detail's recommendation that the Senate alone be given the power to make treaties drew considerable opposition. Mason said it would enable the Senate to "sell the whole country by means of treaties." Madison thought the president, representing the whole people, should have the power. Gouverneur Morris argued for a provision that "no treaty shall be binding . . . which is not ratified by a law." Southern delegates were especially concerned about preventing abandonment by treaty of free navigation of the Mississippi River.

The issue was referred to the Special Committee on Postponed Matters, which recommended vesting the president with the power to make treaties, subject to the advice and consent of two-thirds of the senators present. The latter provision provoked extended debate. On September 7 the convention voted to except peace treaties from the two-thirds rule. Madison then moved to allow two-thirds of the Senate alone to make peace treaties, arguing that the president "would necessarily derive so much power and importance from a state of war that he might be tempted, if authorized, to impede a treaty of peace." The motion was rejected, but after further debate on the advantages and disadvantages of permitting a majority of the Senate to approve a peace treaty, the convention reversed itself and made all treaties subject to the concurrence of a two-thirds vote of the senators present.

Veto Power. The Virginia Plan had proposed joining the judiciary with the executive in exercising the power to veto acts of the legislature, subject to a vote in the Congress on overriding vetoes. Since it was expected that the judiciary would have to pass on the constitutionality of legislation, most delegates thought it improper to give the judiciary a share of the veto power; the proposal was rejected.

Wilson and Alexander Hamilton favored giving the executive an absolute veto, but on June 4 the delegates voted for Gerry's motion, based on the Massachusetts Constitution, for a veto that could be overridden by two-thirds of each branch of the legislature.

When this provision was reconsidered on August 15, it was in the context of a plan to give Congress the power to elect the president, to impeach him and to appoint judges. Many delegates then agreed with Wilson that such an arrangement did not give "a sufficient self-defensive power either to the Executive or Judiciary Department," and the convention voted to require a vote of three-fourths of each chamber to override a veto. But on September 12, after having adopted the presidential elector plan and other changes proposed by the special committee, the convention restored the earlier two-thirds requirement.

The veto power, incorporated in Section 7 of Article I, established the procedure for the enactment of a bill with or without the president's signature. This section also made provision for the "pocket veto" of a bill when "the Congress by their Adjournment prevent its return, in which Case it shall not become Law." Although some delegates indicated a belief that the two-thirds provision was intended to apply to the entire membership of the House and Senate, a two-thirds vote of those present and voting came to be accepted in practice.

THE JUDICIARY

Article III of the Constitution, relating to "the judicial Power of the United States," was developed in the convention with relative ease. The Virginia Plan called for "one or more supreme tribunals" and inferior tribunals to be appointed by the national legislature to try all cases involving crimes at sea, foreigners and citizens of different states, "collection of the National revenue," impeachments and "questions which may involve the national peace and harmony." The convention went on to spell out the jurisdiction of these courts in greater detail, but the only basic changes made in the plan were to vest initially in the Senate and then in the presidency the power to appoint judges, and to transfer the trial of impeachments from the Supreme Court to the Senate.

Lower Courts and Appointment of Judges

Without debate, the delegates agreed to one Supreme Court, but some objected to the establishment of any lower courts. John Rutledge thought the state courts should hear all cases in the first instance, "the right of appeal to the Supreme National Tribunal being sufficient to secure the National rights and uniformity of judgments." Roger Sherman deplored the extra expense. But James Madison argued that without lower courts "dispersed throughout the Republic, with final jurisdiction in many cases, appeals would be multiplied to an oppressive degree." Edmund Randolph said the state courts "cannot be trusted with the administration of the National laws." As a compromise, the convention agreed to permit Congress to decide whether to "ordain and establish" lower courts.

The proposal that the national legislature appoint the judiciary was based on similar provisions in most of the state constitutions. James

Wilson, arguing that "intrigue, partiality and concealment" would result from such a method, proposed appointment by the president. Madison urged appointment by the Senate as "a less numerous and more select body," and this plan was approved on June 13. Although a proposal that the president appoint judges "by and with the advice and consent of the Senate" was defeated by a tie vote July 18, it was adopted in September as part of the compromise that moved the trial of impeachments from the Supreme Court to the Senate.

Tenure and Jurisdiction

Both the Virginia Plan and the New Jersey Plan provided that judges would hold office "during good behaviour" — a rule long considered essential to maintaining the independence of the judiciary. When this provision was considered August 27, John Dickinson proposed that judges "may be removed by the Executive on the application by the Senate and the House of Representatives." Others objected strongly, Wilson contending that "the Judges would be in a bad situation if made to depend on every gust of faction which might prevail in two branches of our Government." Only Connecticut voted for the proposal. The convention also agreed to tenure during good behavior.

Section 2 of Article III specified the cases to which "the judicial Power shall extend" and placed these cases under either the original or appellate jurisdiction of the Supreme Court. Most of the provisions embodied in the section were presented in the August 6 report of the Committee of Detail and adopted by the convention on August 27 with little debate. The most important modification was in the committee's first provision — extending jurisdiction to "all cases arising under the laws" of the United States. Here, the convention amended the language to read: "all cases arising under the Constitution and the laws." This change made it clear that the Supreme Court ultimately was to decide all questions of constitutionality, whether arising in state or federal courts.

Article III did not explicitly authorize the court to pass on the constitutionality of acts of Congress, but the convention clearly anticipated the exercise of that power as one of the acknowledged functions of the courts. Several delegates noted that state courts had "set aside" laws in conflict with the state constitutions. The convention debated at great length, and rejected four times, a proposal to link the court with the president in the veto power. Wilson favored it because "laws may be unjust, may be unwise, may be dangerous, may be destructive, and yet may not be so unconstitutional as to justify the judges in refusing to give them effect." George Mason agreed that the court "could declare an unconstitutional law void."

Supremacy Clause

The role of the judiciary in determining the constitutionality of laws also was implicit in the provision, incorporated in Article VI, which asserted that the Constitution, the laws and the treaties of the United States "shall be the supreme Law of the Land." This provision first appeared on July 17 after the convention had reversed itself and voted to deny Congress the proposed power. Anxious to place some restraint on the free-wheeling state legislatures, the convention adopted instead a substitute offered by Luther Martin and drawn directly from the New Jersey Plan of June 14.

The substitute provided that the laws and treaties of the United States "shall be the supreme law of the respective States, as far as those acts or treaties shall relate to the said States, or their citizens and inhabitants — and that the Judiciaries of the several States shall be bound thereby in their decisions, anything in the respective laws of the individual States to the contrary notwithstanding."

In its report of August 6, the Committee of Detail dropped the qualifying phrase "as far as those acts or treaties shall relate to the said States." The committee then made two other changes. It substituted the word "Judges" for "Judiciaries" in the next clause and the words "Constitutions or laws" for "laws" in the final proviso.

The convention agreed to these and other modifications August 23 and then prefaced the entire provision with the words, "This Constitution." Further revision by the Committee of Style changed "supreme law of the several States" to "supreme law of the land." The effect of the various changes was to make it clear that all judges, state and federal, were bound to uphold the supremacy of the Constitution over all other acts. As finally worded, the "supremacy" clause of Article VI stated:

> *This Constitution, and the laws of the United States which shall be made in Pursuance thereof; and all Treaties made, or which shall be made, under the Authority of the United States, shall be the supreme Law of the Land; and the Judges in every State shall be bound thereby, any Thing in the Constitution or Laws of any State to the Contrary notwithstanding.*

The supremacy clause was reinforced by a further provision in Article VI stating that all members of Congress and of the state legislatures, as well as all executive and judicial officers of the national and state governments, "shall be bound by Oath or Affirmation to support this Constitution."

Limits on Powers of the States

The supremacy clause was designed to prevent the states from passing laws contrary to the Constitution. Since the framers of the Constitution also intended to specify the powers granted to Congress, those powers by implication were denied to the states. By the same reasoning, however, any powers not specifically granted to Congress remained with the states.

To eliminate any doubt of their intention to put an end to irresponsible acts of the individual states, the delegates decided to specify what the states could not do as well as what the states were required to do. Acts prohibited to the states were placed in Section 10 of Article I, while those required of them were placed in Sections 1 and 2 of Article IV.

Most of these provisions — many of which were taken from the Articles of Confederation — were proposed by the Committee of Detail and adopted by the convention on August 28 with little debate or revision. The committee had proposed that the states be required to use gold or silver as legal tender unless Congress gave its consent to another medium of exchange, but the convention voted for an absolute prohibition on other forms of legal tender, Sherman saying the times presented "a favorable crisis for crushing paper money." The convention also added a provision, drawn from the Northwest Ordinance, aimed at the welter of state laws favoring debtors over creditors: no state was to pass any ex post facto law or law impairing the obligation of contracts.

The provisions of Article IV requiring each state to give "full faith and credit" to the acts of other states, to respect "all Privileges and Immunities" of all citizens, and to deliver up fugitives from justice were derived from the Articles of Confederation. To these the convention, at the suggestion of southerners, added a provision that became known as the "fugitive slave" clause; it required such persons to be "delivered up on Claim of the Party to whom such Service or Labour may be due." As with the rest of the Constitution, the enforcement of these provisions in Article IV was assigned, by the supremacy clause, to the courts.

AMENDMENT AND RATIFICATION

A major reason for calling the Constitutional Convention had been that the method for amending the Articles of Confederation — requiring the unanimous consent of the states — had proved to be impractical. So there was general agreement that it was better to provide a process for amending the Constitution "in an easy, regular and constitutional way, than to trust to chance and violence," as George Mason put it. But the formula for doing so received little consideration until the final days of the convention.

The Committee of Detail first proposed that the legislatures of two-thirds of the states have the sole power to initiate amendments by petitioning Congress to call a convention for that purpose. Debate on this provision, adopted August 30, was brief; no one supported the argument of Gouverneur Morris that Congress also should have the power to call a convention. But when the convention reconsidered the issue September 10, Alexander Hamilton raised several objections. "The State Legislatures will not apply for alterations but with a view to increase their own powers," he said, arguing that "the National Legislature will be the first to perceive and will be the most sensible to the necessity of amendments." Hamilton proposed that two-thirds of the Senate and House also be given the power to call a convention."

James Wilson moved that amendments to the Constitution be considered adopted when they had been ratified by two-thirds of the states. When that proposal was defeated, six states to five, Wilson moved to substitute ratification by three-fourths of the states, which was approved without dissent. The convention then adopted a new process, providing that Congress shall propose amendments "whenever two-thirds of both Houses shall deem necessary or on the application of two-thirds" of the state legislatures, and that such amendments would become valid when ratified by either the legislatures or conventions of three-fourths of the states depending on which mode of ratification Congress directed.

Under this formula, any constitutional amendment proposed by two-thirds of the states would be submitted directly to the states for ratification. This was modified September 15 on a motion by Gouverneur Morris. His revision gave Congress the authority, on the application of two-thirds of the states, to "call a Convention for proposing Amendments." Thus, as finally drafted, Article V provided that, in proposing amendments, Congress would act directly while the states would act indirectly. In either case, however, amendments would take effect when approved by three-fourths of the states.

While working out these terms, the convention was forced to restrict the amending power. As a concession to the South, the convention already had barred Congress from outlawing the slave trade before 1808 and from levying any direct tax unless it was in proportion to a count of all whites and three-fifths of the black population (Article I, Section 9). But John Rutledge of South Carolina noted that there was nothing in the proposed article on the amending process to prevent adoption of a constitutional amendment outlawing the slave trade before 1808. He said the slave provisions "might be altered by the States not interested in that property and prejudiced against them" and that he could never agree to such an amending power. So on September 10 it was agreed without debate to add to Article V the proviso that no amendment adopted before 1808 "shall in any manner affect" those two provisions of Article I.

Roger Sherman now worried that "three fourths of the States might be brought to do things fatal to particular States, as abolishing them altogether or depriving them of their equality in the Senate." He proposed, as a further proviso to the amending power, that "No state shall without its consent be affected in its internal police, or deprived of its equal suffrage in the Senate." The term "internal police" covered much more than most delegates were prepared to exclude, and only three states supported Sherman. But the more limited proviso that "no State, without its Consent, shall be deprived of its equal suffrage in the Senate" was accepted without debate and added at the end of Article V.

Campaign for Ratification

According to the resolution of Congress, the Philadelphia convention was to meet for the "sole and express purpose of revising the Articles of Confederation and reporting to Congress and the several legislatures" its recommendations. But the nationalists who organized the convention were determined that the fate of the new Constitution not be entrusted to the state legislatures. The Constitution, they insisted, should be considered "by the supreme authority of the people themselves," as James Madison put it. The legislatures, he pointed out, were in any event without power to consent to changes that "would make essential inroads on the State Constitutions."

By "the people themselves" the nationalists meant special conventions elected for the purpose. Conventions would be more representative than the legislatures, which excluded "many of the ablest men," they argued. The people would be more likely than the state legislatures to favor the Constitution because, according to Rufus King, the legislatures, which would "lose power [under the Constitution] will be most likely to raise objections." Opposing this view were Oliver Ellsworth, who thought conventions were "better fitted to pull down than to build up Constitutions," and Elbridge Gerry, who said the people "would never agree on anything." But the convention rejected Ellsworth's motion for ratification by the legislatures and agreed July 23, by a vote of nine states to one, that the Constitution should be submitted to popularly elected state conventions.

This decision was followed on August 31 by another crucial agreement: the Constitution should enter into force when approved by the conventions of nine of the 13 states. By this time, only a few of the delegates still felt, as Luther Martin did, that "unanimity was necessary to dissolve the existing Confederacy." Seven and ten states also were proposed as minimums, but nine was chosen as the more familiar figure, being the number required to act on important matters under the Articles of Confederation. It also was clearly impractical to require (as the Committee of Detail had proposed) that the Constitution be submitted to the existing Congress "for their approbation," so it was agreed to strike out that provision.

Edmund Randolph and Mason — two of the three delegates who would refuse to sign the Constitution — continued to argue that the document, along with any amendments proposed by the state conventions, should be submitted to another general convention before any final action on it was taken. This proposal to extend the already lengthy constitutional debate generated little enthusiasm among the delegates. Few believed another convention could improve the Constitution significantly. On September 13 Randolph and Mason's proposal was unanimously rejected. As finally drafted, Article VII provided simply that "the Ratification of the Conventions of nine States shall be sufficient for the Establishment of this Constitution between the States so ratifying the Same."

By a separate resolution adopted September 17, it was agreed by the convention that the Constitution should "be laid before the United States in Congress assembled," and that it should then be submitted to "a Convention of Delegates, chosen in each State by the People thereof." As soon as nine states had ratified, the resolution continued, the Congress should set a day for the election of presidential electors, senators and representatives and "the Time and Place for commencing Proceedings under this Constitution."

On September 17, 1787, after nearly four months of debate, the convention adjourned. Ten days later the Congress of the Confederation submitted the Constitution to the states for their consideration, and the struggle for ratification began. Ironically, those who had argued successfully in the convention for a national rather than merely a federal system, and who now took the lead in urging ratification, called themselves Federalists, although there was no reference to anything federal in the Constitution. Those who opposed the Constitution became known as the Anti-Federalists, although the sentiments they espoused had been forming for several years before the fight over ratification.

These two factions, out of which the first political parties in the United States were formed, tended to reflect long-standing divisions among Americans between commercial and agrarian interests, creditors and debtors, men of great or little property, tidewater planters and the small farmers of the interior. But there were important and numerous exceptions to the tendency of Federalists and Anti-Federalists to divide along class, sectional and economic lines. Among the Anti-Federalists were some of the wealthiest and most influential men of the times, including George Mason, Patrick Henry, Richard Henry Lee, George Clinton and James Winthrop.

The Federalists seized the initiative in the ratification process as they had earlier in initiating the convention in Philadelphia. The ensuing campaign of political maneuver, persuasion and propaganda was intense and bitter. Both sides questioned the motives of the other and exaggerated the dire consequences that would ensue if the opposing course were followed. All Anti-Federalists, wrote Ellsworth, were either "men who have lucrative and influential State offices" or "tories, debtors in desperate circumstances, or insurgents." To Luther Martin, the object of the Federalists was "the total abolition of all State Governments and the erection on their ruins of one great and extreme empire."

All of the newspapers of the day published extensive correspondence on the virtues and vices of the new plan of government. The fullest and strongest case for the Constitution was presented in a series of letters written by Madison, Hamilton and Jay under the name of "Publius." Seventy-seven of the letters were published in New York City newspapers between October 27, 1787, and April 4, 1788, and in book form (along with eight additional letters) as *The Federalist*, on May 28, 1788. These letters probably had only a small influence on ratification, but *The Federalist* came to be regarded as the classic exposition of the Constitution as well as one of the most important works on political theory ever written.

Political maneuvers were common in both camps. In Pennsylvania, Federalists moved to call a convention before Congress had officially submitted the Constitution. Nineteen Anti-Federalists thereupon withdrew from the assembly, thus depriving it of a quorum, until a mob seized two of them and dragged them back. When the Massachusetts convention met, the Anti-Federalists were in the majority until John Hancock, the president of that state's constitutional convention, was won over to the Federalist side by promises of support for the new post of vice president of the United States.

Many questions were raised about the new Constitution. Why did the convention fail to draft a Bill of Rights? Would an elected president, with no limit on the number of terms he could serve, lean towards monarchy? Would a strong central government lead to the consolidation and destruction of the separate states? Anti-Federalists accused supporters of the Constitution of trying deliberately to end state sovereignty. They also charged that in drafting the Constitution the Federalists hoped to establish a small ruling class that would protect their economic interests.

In response, Federalists quickly pledged to amend the Constitution to include a Bill of Rights. The fear of monarchy was mitigated by a widespread assumption — held also in the convention — that George Washington would become the first president. This assumption, together with the fact that most Americans knew Washington and Benjamin Franklin supported the Constitution, contributed greatly to the success of the ratification campaign.

The Delaware convention was the first to ratify, unanimously, on December 7, 1787. Then came Pennsylvania, by a 46 to 23 vote, on December 12; New Jersey, unanimously, on December 18; Georgia, unanimously, on January 2, 1788; Connecticut, by a 128 to 40 vote, on January 9, 1788; Massachusetts, 187 to 168, on February 6; Maryland, 63 to 11, on April 28; South Carolina, 149 to 73, on May 23; and New Hampshire, 57 to 46, on June 21. This met the requirement for approval by nine states, but it was clear that without the approval of Virginia and New York the Constitution would stand on shaky ground.

In Virginia, according to Ellsworth, "the opposition wholly originated in two principles: the madness of Mason, and enmity of the Lee faction to Gen. Washington." But Randolph, who had refused with Mason and Gerry to sign the Constitution, eventually was per-

The Federalist Papers

The Federalist Papers, a collection of 85 letters to the public signed with a pseudonym, Publius, appeared at short intervals in the newspapers of New York City beginning on October 27, 1787. The identity of Publius was a secret until several years after publication. In March 1788 the first 36 letters were issued in a collected edition. A second volume of letters containing numbers 37 to 85 was published in May 1788.

The idea for *The Federalist* letters came from Alexander Hamilton who wanted to wage a literary campaign to explain the proposed Constitution and build support for it. James Madison and John Jay agreed to work with him.

Of the 85 letters, Hamilton wrote 56; Madison, 21; and Jay, five. Hamilton and Madison collaborated on three. Jay's low productivity was due to a serious illness in the fall of 1787.

The essays probably had only a small impact on the ratification of the Constitution. Even the most widely circulated newspapers did not travel far in 1788. But they gained importance later as a classic exposition of the Constitution.

Professor Clinton Rossiter in an introduction to the papers described their significance in American political history:

> *The Federalist* is the most important work in political science that has ever been written, or is likely ever to be written, in the United States. It is, indeed, the one product of the American mind that is rightly counted among the classics of political theory. . . . *The Federalist* stands third only to the Declaration of Independence and the Constitution itself among all the sacred writing of American political history. *

* *The Federalist Papers*, with an introduction by Clinton Rossiter (New York: Mentor, 1961), p. vii.

suaded to support it, and on June 25 the Federalists prevailed by a vote of 89 to 79.

New York finally ratified on July 26 by an even narrower margin of 30 to 27, after Hamilton and Jay had threatened that otherwise New York City would secede and join the Union as a separate state. North Carolina on August 4, 1788, first rejected the Constitution by a vote of 75 to 193. It was not until November 21, 1789, that it reversed its earlier vote and ratified the Constitution. Rhode Island — which had not taken part in the Constitutional Convention — by a vote of 34 to 32 on May 29, 1790, became the last of the 13 original states to ratify.

In accordance with the request of the constitutional convention, the Congress of the Confederation on September 13, 1788, designated New York City as the seat of the new government, the first Wednesday of January 1789 as the day for choosing presidential electors, the first Wednesday of February for the meeting of electors, and the first Wednesday of March for the opening session of the first Congress under the new Constitution.

The First Elections

The Constitution empowered the state legislatures to prescribe the method of choosing their presidential electors as well as the time, place and manner of electing their representatives and senators. Virginia and Maryland put the choice of electors directly to the people; in Massachusetts, two were chosen at large and the other eight were picked by the legislature from 24 names submitted by the voters of the eight congressional districts. In the other states, the electors were chosen by the legislature.

In New York, where the Federalists controlled the state Senate and the Anti-Federalists dominated the Assembly, the two houses became deadlocked on the question of acting by joint or concurrent vote. The legislature adjourned without choosing electors.

Election to the House of Representatives also involved a number of spirited contests between Federalists and Anti-Federalists, although the total vote cast in these first elections, estimated to be between 75,000 and 125,000, was a small fraction of the free population of 3.2 million. In Massachusetts and Connecticut, several elections were required in some districts before a candidate obtained a majority of the popular vote. (In the 19th century, five of the New England states required a majority vote to win election to the House; all such requirements had been phased out by the 1890s.) Elbridge Gerry, who had refused to sign the Constitution, finally beat Nathaniel Gorham, also a delegate to the Philadelphia convention, after saying he no longer opposed it. In New Jersey the law did not fix a time for closing the polls, and they stayed open for three weeks. When the House organized for the First Congress, the elections of all four New Jersey representatives were contested.

On March 4, 1789, the day fixed for the new Congress to begin its work, only 13 of the 59 representatives and eight of the 22 senators had arrived in New York City. (Seats allotted to North Carolina and Rhode Island were not filled until 1790, after those states had ratified the Constitution.) It was not until April 1 that a 30th representative arrived to make a quorum of the House; the Senate attained its quorum of 12 on April 6. The two houses then met jointly for the first time to count the electoral vote.

As everyone had assumed, each of the 69 electors had cast one vote for George Washington, who thus became president by unanimous choice. (Four additional electors — two from Maryland and two from Virginia — failed to show up on February 4 to vote.) Of 11 other men among whom the electors distributed their second vote, John Adams received the highest number — 34 — and was declared vice president.

Adams arrived in New York on April 21, Washington on the 23rd and the Inaugural took place on the 30th. Washington took the oath of office prescribed by the Constitution on the balcony of Federal Hall, New York's former City Hall, which housed the president and both houses of Congress until the government moved to Philadelphia in 1790. The president then went to the Senate chamber to deliver a brief inaugural address, in the course of which he declined to accept whatever salary Congress might confer on the office. Thus, by April 30, 1789, the long task of designing and installing a new government for the 13 states had been completed. The Constitution had been, in the words of Gouverneur Morris, "the subject of infinite investigation, disputation and declamation." "While some have boasted it as a work from Heaven," he wrote, "others have given it a less righteous origin. I have many reasons to believe that it is the work of plain, honest men, and such I think it will appear."

ORGANIZATION OF THE
CONSTITUTION OF THE UNITED STATES

The original Constitution (Ratified by June 1788)

The Preamble

Article 1   The Legislative Department
Article 2   The Executive Department
Article 3   The Judicial Department
Article 4   Relations Between the States
Article 5   The Amendment Process
Article 6   General Provisions, Supremacy of Constitution
Article 7   Ratification of the Constitution

The Bill of Rights (Ratified 1791)

1 Freedom of religion, speech, press, assembly, petition
2 Militia and right to bear arms
3 Quartering of troops
4 Searches and seizures
5 Rights of accused persons
6 Criminal trials
7 Jury trials in common law cases
8 Reasonable bail and punishment
9 Rights reserved to the people
10 Powers reserved to the states

Later amendments

11 Suits against states (1795)
12 Elections of President and Vice-President (1804)
13 Slavery abolished (1865)
14 Protections, privileges of citizens of states (1868)
15 Voting rights of all races (1870)
16 Income tax power granted to Congress (1913)
17 Election of senators by the people (1913)
18 Prohibition of intoxicating beverages (1919)
19 Right to vote guaranteed to both sexes (1920)
20 "Lame duck" session of Congress eliminated (1933)
21 Repeal of eighteenth amendment (1933)
22 Limit on President's terms of office (1951)
23 Voting rights for District of Columbia (1961)
24 Prohibition on poll tax (1964)
25 Provision for disability of President (1967)
26 Voting age of eighteen (1971)

THE CONSTITUTION OF THE UNITED STATES

The Preamble

We the People of the United States, in Order to form a more perfect Union, establish Justice, insure domestic Tranquility, provide for the common defence, promote the general Welfare, and secure the Blessings of Liberty to ourselves and our Posterity, do ordain and establish this Constitution for the United States of America.

Article I

Section 1

All legislative Powers herein granted shall be vested in a Congress of the United States, which shall consist of a Senate and House of Representatives.

Section 2

1. The House of Representatives shall be composed of Members chosen every second Year by the People of the several States, and the Electors in each State shall have the Qualifications requisite for Electors of the most numerous Branch of the State Legislature.

2. No Person shall be a Representative who shall not have attained to the age of twenty five Years, and been seven Years a Citizen of the United States, and who shall not, when elected, be an Inhabitant of that State in which he shall be chosen.

3. [Representatives and direct Taxes shall be apportioned among the several States which may be included within this Union, according to their respective Numbers, which shall be determined by adding to the whole Number of free Persons, including those bound to Service for a Term of Years, and excluding Indians not taxed, three fifths of all other Persons.] [1] The actual Enumeration shall be made within three Years after the first Meeting of the Congress of the United States, and within every subsequent Term of ten Years, in such Manner as they shall by Law direct. The Number of Representatives shall not exceed one for every thirty Thousand, but each State shall have at Least one Representative; and until such enumeration shall be made, the State of

55

New Hampshire shall be entitled to chuse three, Massachusetts eight, Rhode-Island and Providence Plantations one, Connecticut five, New-York six, New Jersey four, Pennsylvania eight, Delaware one, Maryland six, Virginia ten, North Carolina five, South Carolina five, and Georgia three.

4. When vacancies happen in the Representation from any State, the Executive Authority thereof shall issue Writs of Election to fill such Vacancies.

5. The House of Representatives shall chuse their Speaker and other Officers; and shall have the sole Power of Impeachment.

Section 3

1. The Senate of the United States shall be composed of two Senators from each State, [chosen by the Legislature thereof,] [2] for six Years; and each Senator shall have one Vote.

2. Immediately after they shall be assembled in Consequence of the first Election, they shall be divided as equally as may be into three Classes. The Seats of the Senators of the first Class shall be vacated at the Expiration of the second Year, of the second Class at the Expiration of the fourth Year, and of the third Class at the Expiration of the sixth Year, so that one third may be chosen every second Year; [and if Vacancies happen by Resignation, or otherwise, during the Recess of the Legislature of any State, the Executive thereof may make temporary Appointments until the next Meeting of the Legislature, which shall then fill such Vacancies.] [3]

3. No Person shall be a Senator who shall not have attained to the Age of thirty Years, and been nine Years a Citizen of the United States, and who shall not, when elected, be an Inhabitant of that State for which he shall be chosen.

4. The Vice President of the United States shall be President of the Senate, but shall have no Vote, unless they be equally divided.

5. The Senate shall chuse their other Officers, and also a President pro tempore, in the Absence of the Vice President, or when he shall exercise the Office of President of the United States.

6. The Senate shall have the sole Power to try all Impeachments. When sitting for that Purpose, they shall be on Oath or Affirmation. When the President of the United States is tried the Chief Justice shall preside: And no Person shall be convicted without the Concurrence of two thirds of the Members present.

7. Judgment in Cases of Impeachment shall not extend further than to removal from Office, and disqualification to hold and enjoy any

Office of honor, Trust or Profit under the United States: but the Party convicted shall nevertheless be liable and subject to Indictment, Trial, Judgment and Punishment, according to Law.

Section 4

1. The Times, Places and Manner of holding Elections for Senators and Representatives, shall be prescribed in each State by the Legislature thereof; but the Congress may at any time by Law make or alter such Regulations, except as to the Places of chusing Senators.

2. The Congress shall assemble at least once in every Year, and such Meeting shall [be on the first Monday in December],[4] unless they shall by Law appoint a different Day.

Section 5

1. Each House shall be the Judge of the Elections, Returns and Qualifications of its own Members, and a Majority of each shall constitute a Quorum to do Business; but a smaller Number may adjourn from day to day, and may be authorized to compel the Attendance of absent Members, in such Manner, and under such Penalties as each House may provide.

2. Each House may determine the Rules of its Proceedings, punish its Members for disorderly Behaviour, and, with the Concurrence of two thirds, expel a Member.

3. Each House shall keep a Journal of its Proceedings, and from time to time publish the same, excepting such Parts as may in their Judgment require Secrecy; and the Yeas and Nays of the Members of either House on any question shall, at the Desire of one fifth of those Present, be entered on the Journal.

4. Neither House, during the Session of Congress, shall, without the Consent of the other, adjourn for more than three days, nor to any other Place than that in which the two Houses shall be sitting.

Section 6

1. The Senators and Representatives shall receive a Compensation for their Services, to be ascertained by Law, and paid out of the Treasury of the United States. They shall in all Cases, except Treason, Felony and Breach of the Peace, be privileged from Arrest during their Attendance at the Session of their respective Houses, and in going to and returning from the same; and for any Speech or Debate in either House, they shall not be questioned in any other Place.

2. No Senator or Representative shall, during the Time for which he was elected, be appointed to any civil Office under the Authority of

the United States, which shall have been created, or the Emoluments whereof shall have been encreased during such time; and no Person holding any Office under the United States, shall be a Member of either House during his Continuance in Office.

Section 7

1. All Bills for raising Revenue shall originate in the House of Representatives; but the Senate may propose or concur with amendments as on other Bills.

2. Every Bill which shall have passed the House of Representatives and the Senate, shall, before it become a Law, be presented to the President of the United States; If he approve he shall sign it, but if not he shall return it, with his Objections to that House in which it shall have originated, who shall enter the Objections at large on their Journal, and proceed to reconsider it. If after such Reconsideration two thirds of that House shall agree to pass the Bill, it shall be sent, together with the Objections, to the other House, by which it shall likewise be reconsidered, and if approved by two thirds of that House, it shall become a Law. But in all such Cases the Votes of both Houses shall be determined by yeas and Nays, and the Names of the Persons voting for and against the Bill shall be entered on the Journal of each House respectively. If any Bill shall not be returned by the President within ten Days (Sunday excepted) after it shall have been presented to him, the Same shall be a Law, in like Manner as if he had signed it, unless the Congress by their Adjournment prevent its Return, in which Case it shall not be a Law.

3. Every Order, Resolution, or Vote to which the Concurrence of the Senate and House of Representatives may be necessary (except on a question of Adjournment) shall be presented to the President of the United States; and before the Same shall take Effect, shall be approved by him, or being disapproved by him, shall be repassed by two thirds of the Senate and House of Representatives, according to the Rules and Limitations prescribed in the Case of a Bill.

Section 8

1. The Congress shall have Power To lay and collect Taxes, Duties, Imposts and Excises, to pay the Debts and provide for the common Defence and general Welfare of the United States; but all Duties, Imposts and Excises shall be uniform throughout the United States;

2. To borrow Money on the credit of the United States;

3. To regulate Commerce with foreign Nations, and among the several States, and with the Indian Tribes;

4. To establish an uniform Rule of Naturalization, and uniform Laws on the subject of Bankruptcies throughout the United States;

5. To coin Money, regulate the Value thereof, and of foreign Coin, and fix the Standard of Weights and Measures;

6. To provide for the Punishment of counterfeiting the Securities and current Coin of the United States;

7. To establish Post Offices and post Roads;

8. To promote the Progress of Science and useful Arts, by securing for limited Times to Authors and Inventors the exclusive Right to their respective Writings and Discoveries;

9. To constitute Tribunals inferior to the supreme Court;

10. To define and punish Piracies and Felonies commited on the high Seas, and Offences against the Law of Nations;

11. To declare War, grant Letters of Marque and Reprisal, and make Rules concerning Captures on Land and Water;

12. To raise and support Armies, but no Appropriation of Money to that Use shall be for a longer Term than two Years;

13. To provide and maintain a Navy;

14. To make Rules for the Government and Regulation of the land and naval Forces;

15. To provide for calling forth the Militia to execute the Laws of the Union, suppress Insurrections and repel Invasions;

16. To provide for organizing, arming, and disciplining, the Militia, and for governing such Part of them as may be employed in the Service of the United States, reserving to the States respectively, the Appointment of the Officers, and the Authority of training the Militia according to the discipline prescribed by Congress;

17. To exercise exclusive Legislation in all Cases whatsoever, over such District (not exceeding ten Miles square) as may, by Cession of Particular States, and the Acceptance of Congress, become the Seat of the Government of the United States, and to exercise like Authority over all Places purchased by the Consent of the Legislature of the State in which the Same shall be, for the Erection of Forts, Magazines, Arsenals, dock-Yards, and other needful Buildings; — And

18. To make all Laws which shall be necessary and proper for carrying into Execution the foregoing Powers, and all other Powers vested by this Constitution in the Government of the United States, or in any Department or Officer thereof.

Section 9

1. The Migration or Importation of such Persons as any of the States now existing shall think proper to admit, shall not be prohibited by the Congress prior to the Year one thousand eight hundred and eight, but a Tax or duty may be imposed on such Importation, not exceeding ten dollars for each Person.

2. The Privilege of the Writ of Habeas Corpus shall not be suspended, unless when in Cases of Rebellion or Invasion the public Safety may require it.

3. No Bill of Attainder or ex post facto Law shall be passed.

4. No capitation, or other direct, Tax shall be laid, unless in Proportion to the Census of Enumeration herein before directed to be taken.[5]

5. No Tax or Duty shall be laid on Articles exported from any State.

6. No Preference shall be given by any Regulation of Commerce or Revenue to the Ports of one State over those of another; nor shall Vessels bound to, or from, one State, be obliged to enter, clear or pay Duties in another.

7. No Money shall be drawn from the Treasury, but in Consequence of Appropriations made by Law; and a regular Statement and Account of the Receipts and Expenditures of all public Money shall be published from time to time.

8. No Title of Nobility shall be granted by the United States: And no Person holding any Office of Profit or Trust under them, shall, without the Consent of the Congress, accept of any present, Emolument, Office, or Title, of any kind whatever, from any King, Prince or foreign State.

Section 10

1. No State shall enter into any Treaty, Alliance, or Confederation; grant Letters of Marque and Reprisal; coin Money; emit Bills of Credit; make any Thing but gold and silver Coin a Tender in Payment of Debts; pass any Bill of Attainder, ex post facto Law, or Law impairing the Obligation of Contracts, or grant any Title of Nobility.

2. No State shall, without the Consent of the Congress, lay any Imposts or Duties on Imports or Exports, except what may be absolutely necessary for executing it's inspection Laws: and the net Produce of all Duties and Imposts, laid by any State on Imports or Exports, shall be for the Use of the Treasury of the United States; and all

such Laws shall be subject to the Revision and Controul of the Congress.

3. No State shall, without the Consent of Congress, lay any Duty of Tonnage, keep Troops, or Ships of War in time of Peace, enter into any Agreement or Compact with another State, or with a foreign Power, or engage in War, unless actually invaded, or in such imminent Danger as will not admit of delay.

Article II

Section 1

1. The executive Power shall be vested in a President of the United States of America. He shall hold his Office during the Term of four Years, and, together with the Vice President, chosen for the same Term, be elected, as follows.

2. Each State shall appoint, in such Manner as the Legislature thereof may direct, a Number of Electors, equal to the whole Number of Senators and Representatives to which the State may be entitled in the Congress: but no Senator or Representative, or Person holding an Office of Trust or Profit under the United States, shall be appointed an Elector.

3. [The Electors shall meet in their respective States, and vote by Ballot for two Persons, of whom one at least shall not be an Inhabitant of the same State with themselves. And they shall make a List of all the Persons voted for, and of the Number of Votes for each; which List they shall sign and certify, and transmit sealed to the Seat of the Government of the United States, directed to the President of the Senate. The President of the Senate shall, in the Presence of the Senate and House of Representatives, open all the Certificates, and the Votes shall then be counted. The Person having the greatest Number of Votes shall be the President, if such Number be a Majority of the whole Number of Electors appointed; and if there be more than one who have such Majority, and have an equal Number of Votes, then the House of Representatives shall immediately chuse by Ballot one of them for President; and if no Person have a Majority, then from the five highest on the list the said House shall in like Manner chuse the President. But in chusing the President, the Votes shall be taken by States, the Representation from each State having one Vote; a quorum for this Purpose shall consist of a Member or Members from two thirds of the States, and a Majority of all the States shall be necessary to a Choice. In every Case, after the Choice of the President, the Person having the

greatest Number of Votes of the Electors shall be the Vice President. But if there should remain two or more who have equal Votes, the Senate shall chuse from them by Ballot the Vice President.] [6]

4. The Congress may determine the Time of chusing the Electors, and the Day on which they shall give their Votes; which Day shall be the same throughout the United States.

5. No Person except a natural born Citizen, or a Citizen of the United States, at the time of the Adoption of this Constitution, shall be eligible to the Office of President; neither shall any Person be eligible to that Office who shall not have attained to the Age of thirty five Years, and been fourteen Years a Resident within the United States.

6. In Case of the Removal of the President from Office, or of his Death, Resignation, or Inability to discharge the Powers and Duties of the said Office,[7] the Same shall devolve on the Vice President, and the Congress may by Law provide for the Case of Removal, Death, Resignation or Inability, both of the President and Vice President, declaring what Officer shall then act as President, and such Officer shall act accordingly, until the Disability be removed, or a President shall be elected.

7. The President shall, at stated Times, receive for his Services, a Compensation, which shall neither be encreased nor diminished during the Period for which he shall have been elected, and he shall not receive within that Period any other Emolument from the United States, or any of them.

8. Before he enter on the Execution of his Office, he shall take the following Oath or Affirmation: — "I do solemnly swear (or affirm) that I will faithfully execute the Office of President of the United States, and will to the best of my Ability, preserve, protect and defend the Constitution of the United States."

Section 2

1. The President shall be Commander in Chief of the Army and Navy of the United States, and of the Militia of the several States, when called into the actual Service of the United States; he may require the Opinion, in writing, of the principal Officer in each of the executive Departments, upon any Subject relating to the Duties of their respective Offices, and he shall have Power to grant Reprieves and Pardons for Offenses against the United States, except in Cases of Impeachment.

2. He shall have Power, by and with the Advice and Consent of the Senate, to make Treaties, provided two thirds of the Senators

present concur; and he shall nominate, and by and with the Advice and Consent of the Senate, shall appoint Ambassadors, other public Ministers and Consuls, Judges of the supreme Court, and all other Officers of the United States, whose Appointments are not herein otherwise provided for, and which shall be established by Law: but the Congress may by Law vest the Appointment of such inferior Officers, as they think proper, in the President alone, in the Courts of Law, or in the Heads of Departments.

3. The President shall have Power to fill up all Vacancies that may happen during the Recess of the Senate, by granting Commissions which shall expire at the End of their next Session.

Section 3

He shall from time to time give to the Congress Information of the State of the Union, and recommend to their Consideration such Measures as he shall judge necessary and expedient; he may, on extraordinary Occasions, convene both Houses, or either of them, and in Case of Disagreement between them, with Respect to the Time of Adjournment, he may adjourn them to such Time as he shall think proper; he shall receive Ambassadors and other public Ministers; he shall take Care that the Laws be faithfully executed, and shall Commission all the Officers of the United States.

Section 4

The President, Vice President and all Civil Officers of the United States, shall be removed from office on Impeachment for, and Conviction of, Treason, Bribery, or other high Crimes and Misdemeanors.

Article III

Section 1

The judicial Power of the United States, shall be vested in one supreme Court, and in such inferior Courts as the Congress may from time to time ordain and establish. The Judges, both of the supreme and inferior Courts, shall hold their Offices during good Behaviour, and shall, at stated Times, receive for their Services, a Compensation, which shall not be diminished during their Continuance in Office.

Section 2

1. The judicial Power shall extend to all Cases, in Law and Equity, arising under this Constitution, the Laws of the United States, and Treaties made, or which shall be made, under their Authority; — to all Cases affecting Ambassadors, other public Ministers and Con-

suls; — to all Cases of admiralty and maritime Jurisdiction; — to Controversies to which the United States shall be a Party; — to Controversies between two or more States; — between a State and Citizens of another State;[8] — between Citizens of different States; — between Citizens of the same State claiming Lands under Grants of different States, and between a State, or the Citizens thereof, and foreign States, Citizens or Subjects.[8]

2. In all Cases affecting Ambassadors, other public Ministers and Consuls, and those in which a State shall be Party, the supreme Court shall have original Jurisdiction. In all the other Cases before mentioned, the supreme Court shall have appellate Jurisdiction, both as to Law and Fact, with such Exceptions, and under such Regulations as the Congress shall make.

3. The Trial of all Crimes, except in cases of Impeachment, shall be by Jury; and such Trial shall be held in the State where the said Crimes shall have been committed; but when not committed within any State, the Trial shall be at such Place or Places as the Congress may by Law have directed.

Section 3

1. Treason against the United States, shall consist only in levying War against them, or in adhering to their Enemies, giving them Aid and Comfort. No Person shall be convicted of Treason unless on the Testimony of two Witnesses to the same overt Act, or on Confession in open Court.

2. The Congress shall have Power to declare the Punishment of Treason, but no Attainder of Treason shall work Corruption of Blood, or Forfeiture except during the Life of the Person attainted.

Article IV

Section 1

Full Faith and Credit shall be given in each State to the public Acts, Records, and judicial Proceedings of every other State. And the Congress may by general Laws prescribe the Manner in which such Acts, Records and Proceedings shall be proved, and the Effect thereof.

Section 2

1. The Citizens of each State shall be entitled to all Privileges and Immunities of Citizens in the several States.

2. A Person charged in any State with Treason, Felony, or other Crime, who shall flee from Justice, and be found in another State, shall

on Demand of the executive Authority of the State from which he fled, be delivered up, to be removed to the State having Jurisdiction of the Crime.

3. [No Person held to Service or Labour in one State, under the Laws thereof, escaping into another, shall, in Consequence of any Law or Regulation therein, be discharged from such Service or Labour, but shall be delivered up on Claim of the Party to whom such Service or Labour may be due.]⁹

Section 3

1. New States may be admitted by the Congress into this Union; but no new State shall be formed or erected within the Jurisdiction of any other State; nor any State be formed by the Junction of two or more States, or Parts of States, without the Consent of the Legislatures of the States concerned as well as of the Congress.

2. The Congress shall have Power to dispose of and make all needful Rules and Regulations respecting the Territory or other Property belonging to the United States; and nothing in this Constitution shall be so construed as to Prejudice any Claims of the United States, or of any particular State.

Section 4

The United States shall guarantee to every State in this Union a Republican Form of Government, and shall protect each of them against Invasion; and on Application of the Legislature, or of the Executive (when the Legislature cannot be convened) against domestic Violence.

Article V

The Congress, whenever two thirds of both Houses shall deem it necessary, shall propose Amendments to this Constitution, or, on the Application of the Legislatures of two thirds of the several States, shall call a Convention for proposing Amendments, which, in either Case, shall be valid to all Intents and Purposes, as Part of this Constitution, when ratified by the Legislatures of three fourths of the several States, or by Conventions in three fourths thereof, as the one or the other Mode of Ratification may be proposed by the Congress; Provided [that no Amendment which may be made prior to the Year One thousand eight hundred and eight shall in any Manner affect the first and fourth Clauses in the Ninth Section of the first Article; and]¹⁰ that no State, without its Consent, shall be deprived of its equal Suffrage in the Senate.

Article VI

1. All Debts contracted and Engagements entered into, before the Adoption of this Constitution, shall be as valid against the United States under this Constitution, as under the Confederation.

2. This Constitution, and the Laws of the United States which shall be made in Pursuance thereof; and all Treaties made, or which shall be made, under the Authority of the United States, shall be the supreme Law of the Land; and the Judges in every State shall be bound thereby, any Thing in the Constitution or Laws of any State to the Contrary notwithstanding.

3. The Senators and Representatives before mentioned, and the Members of the several State Legislatures, and all executive and judicial Officers, both of the United States and of the several States, shall be bound by Oath or Affirmation, to support this Constitution; but no religious Test shall ever be required as a Qualification to any Office or public Trust under the United States.

Article VII

The Ratification of the Conventions of nine States, shall be sufficient for the Establishment of this Constitution between the States so ratifying the Same. Done in Convention by the Unanimous Consent of the States present the Seventeenth Day of September in the Year of our Lord one thousand seven hundred and Eighty seven and of the Independence of the United States of America the Twelfth In witness whereof We have hereunto subscribed our Names, George Washington, President and deputy from Virginia.

New Hampshire: John Langdon,
Nicholas Gilman.

Massachusetts: Nathaniel Gorham,
Rufus King.

Connecticut: William Samuel Johnson,
Roger Sherman.

New York: Alexander Hamilton

New Jersey: William Livingston,
David Brearley,
William Paterson,
Jonathan Dayton.

Pennsylvania:	Benjamin Franklin, Thomas Mifflin, Robert Morris, George Clymer, Thomas FitzSimons, Jared Ingersoll, James Wilson, Gouverneur Morris.
Delaware:	George Read, Gunning Bedford Jr., John Dickinson, Richard Bassett, Jacob Broom.
Maryland:	James McHenry, Daniel of St. Thomas Jenifer, Daniel Carroll.
Virginia:	John Blair, James Madison Jr.
North Carolina:	William Blount, Richard Dobbs Spaight, Hugh Williamson.
South Carolina:	John Rutledge, Charles Cotesworth Pinckney, Charles Pinckney, Pierce Butler.
Georgia:	William Few, Abraham Baldwin.

[The language of the original Constitution, not including the Amendments, was adopted by a convention of the states on September 17, 1787, and was subsequently ratified by the states on the following dates: Delaware, December 7, 1787; Pennsylvania, December 12, 1787; New Jersey, December 18, 1787; Georgia, January 2, 1788; Connecticut, January 9, 1788; Massachusetts, February 6, 1788; Maryland, April 28, 1788; South Carolina, May 23, 1788; New Hampshire, June 21, 1788.

Ratification was completed on June 21, 1788.

The Constitution subsequently was ratified by Virginia, June 25, 1788; New York, July 26, 1788; North Carolina, November 21, 1789; Rhode Island, May 29, 1790; and Vermont, January 10, 1791.]

THE AMENDMENTS

Amendment I

(First ten amendments ratified December 15, 1791.)

Congress shall make no law respecting an establishment of religion, or prohibiting the free exercise thereof; or abridging the freedom of speech, or of the press; or the right of the people peaceably to assemble, and to petition the Government for a redress of grievances.

Amendment II

A well regulated Militia, being necessary to the security of a free State, the right of the people to keep and bear Arms, shall not be infringed.

Amendment III

No Soldier shall, in time of peace be quartered in any house, without the consent of the Owner, nor in time of war, but in a manner to be prescribed by law.

Amendment IV

The right of the people to be secure in their persons, houses, papers, and effects, against unreasonable searches and seizures, shall not be violated, and no Warrants shall issue, but upon probable cause, supported by Oath or affirmation, and particularly describing the place to be searched, and the persons or things to be seized.

Amendment V

No person shall be held to answer for a capital, or otherwise infamous crime, unless on a presentment or indictment of a Grand Jury, except in cases arising in the land or naval forces, or in the Militia, when in actual service in time of War or public danger; nor shall any person be subject for the same offence to be twice put in jeopardy of life or limb; nor shall be compelled in any criminal case to be a witness against himself, nor be deprived of life, liberty, or property, without due process of law; nor shall private property be taken for public use, without just compensation.

Amendment VI

In all criminal prosecutions, the accused shall enjoy the right to a speedy and public trial, by an impartial jury of the State and district wherein the crime shall have been committed, which district shall have been previously ascertained by law, and to be informed of the nature and cause of the accusation; to be confronted with the witnesses against him; to have compulsory process for obtaining witnesses in his favor, and to have the Assistance of Counsel for his defence.

Amendment VII

In Suits at common law, where the value in controversy shall exceed twenty dollars, the right of trial by jury shall be preserved, and no fact tried by a jury, shall be otherwise re-examined in any Court of the United States, than according to the rules of the common law.

Amendment VIII

Excessive bail shall not be required, nor excessive fines imposed, nor cruel and unusual punishments inflicted.

Amendment IX

The enumeration in the Constitution, of certain rights, shall not be construed to deny or disparage others retained by the people.

Amendment X

The powers not delegated to the United States by the Constitution, nor prohibited by it to the States, are reserved to the States respectively, or to the people.

Amendment XI *(Ratified February 7, 1795)*

The Judicial power of the United States shall not be construed to extend to any suit in law or equity, commenced or prosecuted against one of the United States by Citizens of another State, or by Citizens or Subjects of any Foreign State.

Amendment XII *(Ratified June 15, 1804)*

The Electors shall meet in their respective states and vote by ballot for President and Vice-President, one of whom, at least, shall not be an inhabitant of the same state with themselves; they shall name in their ballots the person voted for as President, and in distinct ballots the person voted for as Vice-President, and they shall make distinct lists of all persons voted for as President, and of all persons voted for as Vice-President, and of the number of votes for each, which lists they shall sign and certify, and transmit sealed to the seat of the government of the United States, directed to the President of the Senate; — The President of the Senate shall, in the presence of the Senate and House of Representatives, open all the certificates and the votes shall then be counted; — The person having the greatest number of votes for President, shall be the President, if such number be a majority of the whole number of Electors appointed; and if no person have such majority, then from the persons having the highest numbers not exceeding three on the list of those voted for as President, the House of Representatives shall choose immediately, by ballot, the President. But in choosing the President, the votes shall be taken by states, the representation from each state having one vote; a quorum for this purpose shall consist of a member or members from two-thirds of the states, and a majority of all the states shall be necessary to a choice. [And if the House of Representatives shall not choose a President whenever the right of choice shall devolve upon them, before the fourth day of March next following, then the Vice-President shall act as President, as in the case of the death or other constitutional disability of the President —][11] The person having the greatest number of votes as Vice-President, shall be the Vice-President, if such number be a majority of the whole number of Electors appointed, and if no person have a majority, then from the two highest numbers on the list, the Senate shall choose the Vice-President; a quorum for the purpose shall consist of two-thirds of the whole number of Senators, and a majority of the whole number shall be necessary to a choice. But no person constitutionally ineligible to the office of President shall be eligible to that of Vice-President of the United States.

Amendment XIII *(Ratified December 6, 1865)*
Section 1
Neither slavery nor involuntary servitude, except as a punishment for crime whereof the party shall have been duly convicted, shall exist within the United States, or any place subject to their jurisdiction.

Section 2
Congress shall have power to enforce this article by appropriate legislation.

Amendment XIV *(Ratified July 9, 1868)*
Section 1. All persons born or naturalized in the United States and subject to the jurisdiction thereof, are citizens of the United States and of the State wherein they reside. No State shall make or enforce any law which shall abridge the privileges or immunities of citizens of the United States; nor shall any State deprive any person of life, liberty, or property, without due process of law; nor deny to any person within its jurisdiction the equal protection of the laws.

Section 2
Representatives shall be apportioned among the several States according to their respective numbers, counting the whole number of

persons in each State, excluding Indians not taxed. But when the right to vote at any election for the choice of electors for President and Vice President of the United States, Representatives in Congress, the Executive and Judicial officers of a State, or the members of the Legislature thereof, is denied to any of the male inhabitants of such State, being twenty-one years of age,[12] and citizens of the United States, or in any way abridged, except for participation in rebellion, or other crime, the basis of representation therein shall be reduced in the proportion which the number of such male citizens shall bear to the whole number of male citizens twenty-one years of age in such State.

Section 3

No person shall be a Senator or Representative in Congress, or elector of President and Vice President, or hold any office, civil or military, under the United States, or under any State, who, having previously taken an oath, as a member of Congress, or as an officer of the United States, or as a member of any State legislature, or as an executive or judicial officer of any State, to support the Constitution of the United States, shall have engaged in insurrection or rebellion against the same, or given aid or comfort to the enemies thereof. But Congress may by a vote of two-thirds of each House, remove such disability.

Section 4

The validity of the public debt of the United States, authorized by law, including debts incurred for payment of pensions and bounties for services in suppressing insurrection or rebellion, shall not be questioned. But neither the United States nor any State shall assume or pay any debt or obligation incurred in aid of insurrection or rebellion against the United States, or any claim for the loss or emancipation of any slave; but all such debts, obligations and claims shall be held illegal and void.

Section 5

The Congress shall have power to enforce, by appropriate legislation, the provisions of this article.

Amendment XV (Ratified February 3, 1870)
Section 1

The right of citizens of the United States to vote shall not be denied or abridged by the United States or by any State on account of race, color, or previous condition of servitude.

Section 2

The Congress shall have power to enforce this article by appropriate legislation.

Amendment XVI *(Ratified February 3, 1913)*

The Congress shall have power to lay and collect taxes on incomes, from whatever source derived, without apportionment among the several States, and without regard to any census or enumeration.

Amendment XVII *(Ratified April 8, 1913)*

The Senate of the United States shall be composed of two Senators from each State, elected by the people thereof, for six years; and each Senator shall have one vote. The electors in each State shall have the qualifications req␣isite for electors of the most numerous branch of the State legislatures.

When vacancies happen in the representation of any State in the Senate, the executive authority of such State shall issue writs of election to fill such vacancies: *Provided,* That the legislature of any State may empower the executive thereof to make temporary appointments until the people fill the vacancies by election as the legislature may direct.

This amendment shall not be so construed as to affect the election or term of any Senator chosen before it becomes valid as part of the Constitution.

Amendment XVIII *(Ratified January 16, 1919)*

Section 1

After one year from the ratification of this article the manufacture, sale, or transportation of intoxicating liquors within, the importation thereof into, or the exportation thereof from the United States and all territory subject to the jurisdiction thereof for beverage purposes is hereby prohibited.

Section 2

The Congress and the several States shall have concurrent power to enforce this article by appropriate legislation.

Section 3

This article shall be inoperative unless it shall have been ratified as an amendment to the Constitution by the legislatures of the several States, as provided in the Constitution, within seven years from the date of the submission hereof to the States by the Congress.][13]

Amendment XIX *(Ratified August 18, 1920)*

The right of citizens of the United States to vote shall not be denied or abridged by the United States or by any State on account of sex.

Congress shall have power to enforce this article by appropriate legislation.

Amendment XX *(Ratified January 23, 1933)*

Section 1

The terms of the President and Vice President shall end at noon on the 20th day of January, and the terms of Senators and Representatives at noon on the 3d day of January, of the years in which such terms would have ended if this article had not been ratified; and the terms of their successors shall then begin.

Section 2

The Congress shall assemble at least once in every year, and such meeting shall begin at noon on the 3d day of January, unless they shall by law appoint a different day.

Section 3[14]

If, at the time fixed for the beginning of the term of the President, the President elect shall have died, the Vice President elect shall become President. If a President shall not have been chosen before the time fixed for the beginning of his term, or if the President elect shall have failed to qualify, then the Vice President elect shall act as President until a President shall have qualified; and the Congress may by law provide for the case wherein neither a President elect nor a Vice President elect shall have qualified, declaring who shall then act as President, or the manner in which one who is to act shall be selected, and such person shall act accordingly until a President or Vice President shall have qualified.

Section 4

The Congress may by law provide for the case of the death of any of the persons from whom the House of Representatives may choose a President whenever the right of choice shall have devolved upon them, and for the case of the death of any of the persons from whom the Senate may choose a Vice President whenever the right of choice shall have devolved upon them.

Section 5

Sections 1 and 2 shall take effect on the 15th day of October following the ratification of this article.

Section 6

This article shall be inoperative unless it shall have been ratified as an amendment to the Constitution by the legislatures of three-fourths of the several States within seven years from the date of its submission.

Amendment XXI *(Ratified December 5, 1933)*

Section 1

The eighteenth article of amendment to the Constitution of the United States is hereby repealed.

Section 2

The transportation or importation into any State, Territory or possession of the United States for delivery or use therein of intoxicating liquors, in violation of the laws thereof, is hereby prohibited.

Section 3

This article shall be inoperative unless it shall have been ratified as an amendment to the Constitution by conventions in the several States, as provided in the Constitution, within seven years from the date of the submission hereof to the States by the Congress.

Amendment XXII *(Ratified February 27, 1951)*

Section 1

No person shall be elected to the office of the President more than twice, and no person who has held the office of President, or acted as President, for more than two years of a term to which some other person was elected President shall be elected to the office of the President more than once. But this Article shall not apply to any person holding the office of President when this Article was proposed by the Congress, and shall not prevent any person who may be holding the office of President, or acting as President, during the term within which this Article become operative from holding the office of President or acting as President during the remainder of such term.

Section 2

This Article shall be inoperative unless it shall have been ratified as an amendment to the Constitution by the legislatures of three-fourths of the several States within seven years from the date of its submission to the States by the Congress.

Amendment XXIII (Ratified March 29, 1961)
Section 1

The District constituting the seat of Government of the United States shall appoint in such manner as the Congress may direct:

A number of electors of President and Vice President equal to the whole number of Senators and Representatives in Congress to which the District would be entitled if it were a State, but in no event more than the least populous State; they shall be in addition to those appointed by the States, but they shall be considered, for the purposes of the election of President and Vice President, to be electors appointed by a State; and they shall meet in the District and perform such duties as provided by the twelfth article of amendment.

Section 2

The Congress shall have power to enforce this article by appropriate legislation.

Amendment XXIV (Ratified January 23, 1964)
Section 1

The right of citizens of the United States to vote in any primary or other election for President or Vice President, for electors for President or Vice President, or for Senator or Representative in Congress, shall not be denied or abridged by the United States or any State by reason of failure to pay any poll tax or other tax.

Section 2

The Congress shall have power to enforce this article by appropriate legislation.

Amendment XXV (Ratified February 10, 1967)
Section 1

In case of the removal of the President from office or of his death or resignation, the Vice President shall become President.

Section 2

Whenever there is a vacancy in the office of the Vice President, the President shall nominate a Vice President who shall take office upon confirmation by a majority vote of both Houses of Congress.

Section 3

Whenever the President transmits to the President pro tempore of the Senate and the Speaker of the House of Representatives his written declaration that he is unable to discharge the powers and duties of his office, and until he transmits to them a written declaration to the contrary, such powers and duties shall be discharged by the Vice President as Acting President.

Section 4

Whenever the Vice President and a majority of either the principal officers of the executive departments or of such other body as Congress may by law provide, transmit to the President pro tempore of the Senate and the Speaker of the House of Representatives their written declaration that the President is unable to discharge the powers and duties of his office, the Vice President shall immediately assume the powers and duties of the office as Acting President.

Thereafter, when the President transmits to the President pro tempore of the Senate and the Speaker of the House of Representatives his written declaration that no inability exists, he shall resume the powers and duties of his office unless the Vice President and a majority of either the principal officers of the executive department or of such other body as Congress may by law provide, transmit within four days to the President pro tempore of the Senate and the Speaker of the House of Representatives their written declaration that the President is unable to discharge the powers and duties of his office. Thereupon Congress shall decide the issue, assembling within forty-eight hours for that purpose if not in session. If the Congress, within twenty-one days after receipt of the latter written declaration, or, if Congress is not in session, within twenty-one days after Congress is required to assemble, determines by two-thirds vote of both houses that the President is unable to discharge the powers and duties of his office, the Vice President shall continue to discharge the same as Acting President; otherwise, the President shall resume the powers and duties of his office.

Amendment XXVI (Ratified July 1, 1971)

Section 1

The right of citizens of the United States, who are eighteen years of age or older, to vote shall not be denied or abridged by the United States or by any State on account of age.

Section 2

The Congress shall have power to enforce this article by appropriate legislation.

Notes

1. The part in brackets was changed by section 2 of the Fourteenth Amendment.
2. The part in brackets was changed by section 1 of the Seventeenth Amendment.
3. The part in brackets was changed by the second paragraph of the Seventeenth Amendment.
4. The part in brackets was changed by section 2 of the Twentieth Amendment.
5. The Sixteenth Amendment gave Congress the power to tax incomes.
6. The material in brackets has been superseded by the Twelfth Amendment.
7. This provision has been affected by the Twenty-fifth Amendment.
8. These clauses were affected by the Eleventh Amendment.
9. This paragraph has been superseded by the Thirteenth Amendment.
10. Obsolete.
11. The part in brackets has been superseded by section 3 of the Twentieth Amendment.
12. See the Twenty-sixth Amendment.
13. This Amendment was repealed by section 1 of the Twenty-first Amendment.
14. See the Twenty-fifth Amendment.

Source: U.S. Congress, House, Committee on the Judiciary, *The Constitution of the United States of America, As Amended Through July 1971*, H. Doc. 93-215, 93rd Cong., 2nd sess., 1974.

AN INDEX TO THE
CONSTITUTION OF THE UNITED STATES

	Art.	Sect.	Para.
Captures on land and water	I	8	11
Census of population	I	2	3
Checks and balances			
executive on judicial			
grants pardons and reprieves	II	2	1
nominates judges	II	2	2
executive on legislative			
altering President's salary prohibited	II	1	7
recommendations to Congress	II	3	
special sessions of Congress	II	3	
state of union message	II	3	
veto power	I	7	2
judicial on executive			
impeachment trials	I	3	6
judges' term of office	III	1	
judicial review power	(See Note A)		
judicial on legislative			
judges' salaries may not be lowered	III	1	
judges' term of office	III	1	
judicial review power	(See Note A)		
legislative on executive			
confirms President's appointments	II	2	2
consents to President's treaties	II	2	2
controls appropriations	I	7	1
	I	8	1
	I	8	12
establishes executive departments	II	2	2
impeachment power	I	2	5
	I	3	6
	II	4	
investigates executive branch	(See Note B)		
override of President's veto	I	7	2
role in filling office of President	A12		
	A25	4	2
legislative on judicial			
change Court's appellate jurisdiction	III	2	2
change Court's size	(See Note C)		
confirms appointments of judges	II	2	2
determines punishment for treason	III	3	2
establishes, abolishes lower courts	III	1	

E

R

S

W

NOTES

Note A

The Supreme Court's Power of Judicial Review

Courts often are called upon to review cases in which there is a dispute as to whether a law or a government official's action is permitted under the Constitution. The Supreme Court has the final word in such cases. For this reason, the Court is a major factor in the balance of power among the three branches of government established by the Constitution. Under the power of judicial review, for example, the Court may rule on the legality of a town's zoning law, a lower court's conduct of a trial, a school board regulation, or an action by a policeman or the President of the United States.

This power is not provided for directly in the Constitution. The Court itself defined it in 1803 in the case *Marbury versus Madison.* Chief Justice John Marshall wrote the opinion. It declared that judicial review is the outgrowth of English and American legal traditions along with certain provisions of the Constitution itself. The reasoning was that courts first must decide what laws mean in order to rule on cases arising under them; that the Supreme Court must decide the meaning of the Constitution in order to defend it as the "supreme law of the land"; and, finally, it must decide whether a law or action is in agreement with the Constitution, because it may recognize only laws which are made in pursuance of that basic law, according to Article VI, Paragraph 2. If the Court finds that a law or action is not in agreement with the Constitution, it can declare it unconstitutional and unenforceable.

Note B

The Power of Congress to Investigate

In order to carry out its functions, Congress must gather information. Such functions include passing laws on a vast variety of subjects, approving treaties, evaluating individuals nominated by the President, and appropriating money for carrying out the programs of government. Closely associated with this is the authority to require individuals to appear and provide necessary information—the subpoena power.

Although the investigating power is not specifically provided for in the Constitution, it has been considered part of our law-making tradition from the earlier state legislatures and the English Parliament. It is a significant power in the check and balance system. There are limits to it, however. The Supreme Court has said that the Congress may not investigate to restrict the First Amendment rights of individuals or to attempt to exercise powers assigned to the executive and judicial departments.

Note C

The Power of Congress to Change the Size of the Supreme Court

The Constitution says nothing about the size of the Supreme Court or whether it can be changed from time to time. Under Article III, Section 1, Congress established the judicial system in the Judiciary Act of 1789. It established a six-member court. At various times since, the size has been changed to seven, ten, and the present nine members. The Court has made no ruling on the subject.

Background for the notes has been obtained from Edward S. Corwin, and Jack W. Peltason, *Understanding the Constitution* (New York: Holt, Rinehart, & Winston, 1964).

A GLOSSARY OF TERMS IN THE
CONSTITUTION OF THE UNITED STATES

Abridge

To reduce, deprive, or cut off.

To adjourn

To halt a meeting temporarily.

Admiralty

Admiralty laws apply to shipping and disputes and offenses committed on the high seas; also to matters on public waters within the country, such as the Great Lakes.

Affirmation

A solemn declaration that serves for those whose beliefs will not permit the swearing of an oath.

Alliance

An agreement between two or more nations to come to the defense of any partner that is attacked.

To apportion

To divide up or distribute in proportion to something. In this case, the larger the population of a state, the more representatives it has and the more taxes come from it.

Appropriations

Money set aside by government for specific uses, such as military forces or highway construction.

Ascertain

To obtain information.

Attainder

Guilt. A bill of attainder is a law declaring someone guilty of an offense without a trial.

Bankruptcy

Unable to pay one's debts. Bankruptcy laws provide a fair and orderly way to divide up the bankrupt person's remaining property among those to whom money is owed.

Bill of credit

A kind of paper money issued by the states before the Constitution was adopted. The Constitution prohibited states from issuing them so that only Congress would have the power to coin money and regulate its value.

Capital crime

An offense punishable by death.

Capitation tax	A tax put directly upon each person. It takes the same amount from everyone, rich and poor.
Cession	Giving up land to another government.
Commerce	Buying, selling, and transporting goods and services between places, such as states.
Common law	The body of laws that comes from court decisions of the past rather than from written laws. Common law was built up over centuries and represents our legal tradition. It extends back into British history.
Compulsory process	A court's power to order a person to appear in court to testify. In the Sixth Amendment, this power may be used to guarantee that witnesses will testify in behalf of an accused person. The order is called a subpoena (suh-pee-nah).
Concurrence	Agreement.
Confederation	A group of independent states or nations united for mutual advantages but without giving up power to act independently.
To constitute	To establish or bring into being.
Constitution	The fundamental law of an organized group. It establishes its government system and the basic principles guiding its operation.
Construed	Interpreted or understood to have a particular meaning.
To convene	To bring together a group for the purpose of conducting a meeting.
Corruption of blood	"Blood" here means members of a guilty person's family. Corruption of blood means making those family members share in the guilt.
Crime	An offense against society in violation of public law and punishable mainly by death, imprisonment, or fine.
To devolve	To pass authority to someone else. The authority to vote for President is passed to the House of Representatives.

Due process of law	The precautions which the government must take to protect the lives, liberty, and property of individuals when the government is dealing with them.
Duty	A tax on the value of goods shipped, most often, into a country.
Elector	One who has authority to elect someone to an official position — either a citizen in public elections or one who is authorized in the electoral system to cast a vote for President.
Emolument	A salary or fee.
Enumeration	A list of rights or powers.
Equity	Fairness. Settling a dispute which cannot be covered by written laws. Each party states its side, and the court makes a judgment based on what is most reasonable and just.
Ex post facto law	A law that makes something illegal and also provides punishment for those who did it before it was made illegal.
Excise	A tax upon certain products, such as leather goods or jewelry.
Executive	In government, the authority which carries out, or executes, the laws.
Felony	A serious crime that is punished by a longer term of imprisonment than a misdemeanor.
Full faith and credit	The recognition by each state of every other state's official proceedings. For example, one state recognizes the driver's license of an individual from another state as evidence that the person is a qualified driver.
Grand jury	A special jury that decides whether there is enough criminal evidence against a person to formally charge him or her in court.
Grievance	A complaint about something unjust that was done.
Habeas corpus, writ of	A court order requiring authorities to bring into court a person being held by them. The court will

	set a deadline after which the prisoner must either be charged with an offense and scheduled for court appearance, or be set free.
Imminent	Something that threatens to happen very soon.
Immunities	Freedom from, or protection against, unjust government action. The First Amendment freedoms are immunities.
Impeachment	A formal accusation charging a government official with a crime or other serious wrongdoing.
Impost	A tax, especially one paid on goods entering the country.
Indictment	A formal accusation of a serious crime which is voted by a grand jury.
Infamous	Vicious, immoral, evil. A felony is an infamous crime.
Insurrection	Armed uprising against authority, but not as organized and widespread as rebellion.
Involuntary servitude	Forced labor, usually of prison inmates.
Jeopardy	Danger or risk.
Judicial	The function of judging cases that arise under the laws.
Jurisdiction	Authority. The kinds of subjects and geographic area over which an official body has authority to make decisions and take action.
Legislative	The function of making laws.
Maritime	See "Admiralty."
Marque and reprisal	Authorization to private shipowners to attack enemy vessels.
Militia	A body of private citizens organized, trained, and prepared to carry out military activities, but only when called into service by government authorities in emergencies.
Misdemeanor	A crime less serious than a felony that carries a shorter jail sentence, usually less than a year.
Naturalization	The legal process by which an immigrant gets the same rights as a natural born citizen has.

Nobility	A class of people with titles of rank, such as duke or baron, who formerly had special rights that the majority of people did not have.
To ordain	To give authority.
Overt	Open to view.
To petition	To make a formal request.
To prejudice	To unfairly influence the way a person thinks or feels about something.
Presentment	A charge or accusation.
Probable cause	Sufficient reason for investigators to believe that something or someone is in the place to be searched.
Pursuance	"In pursuance thereof" means "in following the rules of" the Constitution.
Pro tempore	A Latin phrase meaning "for the time being."
Quorum	The smallest number of members who must be present for a group to make official decisions.
Ratification	Approval.
Rebellion	Open, organized, widespread efforts to overthrow the government. A more serious threat than an insurrection.
To redress	To correct something that is unjust.
Reprieve	A delay or postponement.
Requisite	Required.
Revenue	Funds collected by government so that it may carry out its functions.
Securities	Stocks, which show a share of ownership in a business, or bonds, which show the amount of debt owed by a business or government to the holder or owner of the bond.
Service	"Held to service" means slavery.
Succeed	Taking over a position of authority after it has been vacated.
Suffrage	The right to vote.
Taxes	Required payments to government.

Tender The way of making payment along with the material itself (gold, silver, bills, etc.)

Tonnage A tax on boats based upon the number of tons of cargo they carry.

Treaty An official agreement between two or more nations.

Tribunal A court or other body which makes judgments.

Warrant An authorization issued by a judge.

Writs of election Orders to hold an election.

Yeas and nays Yes and no votes.

182 5658 7 ym

J